Professional
TOUCHES

Lesley Herbert

MEREHURST
LONDON

To my husband Tony, thank you for all
your love and patience. To mum,
without whose continuous help this book could
not have been written.
Lastly, to my diamonds – Katie and Marc.

A standard spoon measurement is used in all recipes.
1 teaspoon = one 5ml spoon
1 tablespoon = one 15ml spoon
All spoon measures are level.

Quantities are given in metric, Imperial and cups. Follow one set of
measures only as they are not interchangeable. American terms
have been included as necessary throughout, given in brackets
following the UK name. The following are typical equivalent
terms:
glacé cherries – candied cherries
icing sugar – confectioner's sugar
plain flour – all-purpose flour
greaseproof paper – parchment (grease-resistant vegetable
parchment)
icing tubes – icing tips
liquid glucose – clear corn syrup

Published 1991 by Merehurst Limited
Ferry House
51–57 Lacy Road
Putney
London SW15 1PR

Copyright © Merehurst Limited 1991

A catalogue record for this book is available from the British Library
ISBN 1 85391 168 2

Edited by Bridget Jones
Designed by Maggie Aldred
Photography by David Gill

Typeset by Tradespools Ltd, Frome, Somerset
Colour separation by Fotographics, UK – Hong Kong
Printed in Portugal by Printer Portuguesa Indústria Gráfica, Lda.

Contents

INTRODUCTION

The challenge of creating a cake or sugar item to be assessed and judged for competitions has always encouraged me to experiment with new ideas and difficult techniques. Twelve years of competing in bakery, sugarcraft and Salon Culinaire competitions have also provided the opportunity for acquiring a good deal of experience, much of which I have attempted to share with you throughout this book.

Whatever your reasons for decorating cakes at this level, whether for profession or profit, as a hobby or for competition, I hope you will find the designs and skills a source of inspiration! I have used each cake as a platform for demonstrating one, or sometimes more, particular techniques, explained in step-by-step detail. The choice of completing the designs exactly as shown or simply picking up on certain aspects of the work is up to you. When you have mastered each of the main skills you will be able to adapt ideas to build up your own creations.

COMPETITION WORK

Schedule This must be written to give both competitors and judges a clear understanding of what is required. Ambiguous statements have to be avoided. For example 'birthday cake, maximum size 25 cm (10 inch)' could refer to the cake before decorating or the iced cake; it could be taken as the size including the board or collar. It does not cover unusual items such as a hexagonal cake which may be measured from point to point or across the width of the straight sides. However, if the schedule reads: 'Total exhibit must fit into a 25 cm (10 inch) square,' there is no doubt about the size required.

If ever you have to write a schedule, then seek help from the chairman of the judges or from experienced competitors, as providing a good schedule is half-way to ensuring the smooth running of the competition. If you are competing, then read the schedule carefully, looking at all the following details.

Selecting the Classes This is a guide to eligibility. Individual schedules vary so check requirements closely.

Junior Class: Age limit varies, so read the schedule thoroughly.

Novice Class: This class is generally for those who have never won a first prize in a major competition.

Open Class: For competitors who have never previously won a first prize in the class entered. For example, those who have previously won first prize in the sugarpaste cake class, may no longer enter that particular open class again.

Senior or Master Class: For competitors who have won a first prize in an open class.

Table d'Honneur: For exhibits by invited laureates or by competitors who have won three gold medals in any one class at a major competition.

Planning Your Exhibit Read the schedule from cover to cover, then list classes which are of interest. Make a list of all the specifications, for example size, shape, materials and whether off-pieces of artificial decorations are permitted or not. Identify the closing date for entries, the conditions, fee and address of the organisers. If in doubt, contact the organisers for clarification rather than risk being disqualified due to misunderstanding the rules. Look out for ideas for your exhibit, not just from books on cake decorating or photographs but also from cards, flower arrangements and embroidery. Dinner services are among my favourite sources of inspiration as they are decorated with different sizes and shapes of flower sprays all following the same theme.

Do not be tempted to enter too many classes – it is better to devote your full attention to one exhibit. Once you have a design in mind, select an appropriate colour scheme, remembering that you are working with food which must appear to be edible. Select ribbons and food colours carefully before commencing work, as some colours are very difficult to match.

Start to coat the cake or dummy as soon as possible as it will keep perfectly well if stored double-boxed (one cake box inside another to prevent damage, dust or fading). I have learned, to my cost, that a last-minute rush results in undue stress and silly mistakes. If possible, coat two cakes so that you have the best choice of coatings. This also allows you to experiment with different colours and techniques.

Assess your completed exhibit under the following headings: coating; piping; proportion and balance; features (run-outs, flowers etc); colour combinations; and overall effect. Make a note of good and bad points to help with future entries.

Transporting Exhibits Place a small square of thin foam in the bottom of the cake box to prevent the exhibit moving. A sheet of foam in the back of the car stops the box sliding if you have to stop suddenly. A clear note in the back windscreen 'WEDDING CAKE IN TRANSIT' is valuable – it is surprising how courteous people can be while you try to miss all the bumps and holes in the road.

Allow plenty of time to pack and transport your work. Rushing either the packing process or the journey can result in irreparable damage to delicate sugarwork. When you arrive, look around the venue and register before bringing in your exhibit. Place your registration numbers on your entry before positioning it on the required table. Take great care not to disturb or damage other entries.

After the Results I have learned a great deal about the cake decorating from other competitors and judges' comments. I always ask for advice and find it most helpful if the judge can talk through each skill. Of course winning is important, because that is the ultimate aim, but do not put too much importance on it – it is equally vital to learn by the experience of entering.

Take the opportunity to study other exhibits and try to decide why you like or dislike a piece. This way it is possible to learn from other successes or faults. Never speak rudely of a cake – the competitor may well be a six foot tall rugby player, and probably standing behind you! Joking apart, nothing is gained by criticising someone else's achievement and that is what every entry amounts to.

When the results are processed, do not take personal offence if you have not received an award. Do not be discouraged if you do not achieve perfect results first time or if your competition entries do not receive acclaim, just try a little harder next time. Anyone who has won competitions will have discovered a new skill – trophy cleaning! Good luck with all your work, if entering competitions is your aim, remember that without your entries the competitions would not exist.

JOY TO THE WORLD

INGREDIENTS

◆

20 cm (8 inch) round Rich Fruit Cake,
see page 138
apricot jam, boiled and sieved
1 kg (2 lb) marzipan
clear alcohol (gin or vodka)
1 kg (2 lb) sugarpaste
icing (confectioner's) sugar for
rolling out
Stock Syrup, see page 140
about 375 g (12 oz/¾ lb) Royal Icing,
see page 139
selection of food colours
9 Leaves, see page 125
3 Open Roses, see page 126

EQUIPMENT

◆

thin cake board cut to size of cake
greaseproof (parchment) paper
rolling pin
smoothers
28 cm (11 inch) round board
wax paper
scriber
fine paint brush
garrett frill cutter
no. 1 and 0 piping tubes (tips)
1 metre (1 yard) ribbon, 2 mm
(⅛ inch) wide

ORDER OF WORK

◆

This effective design may be adapted to suit any occasion by changing the picture and inscription.

Cover the fruit cake with marzipan and sugarpaste, and leave to dry for about 3 days before decorating. Then set it on a cake board.

Using the template, run-out several oval plaques and allow them to dry under a lamp. Remove the plaques from the wax paper when dry and use the scriber to mark the design on them. Paint the design with food colour. The benefit of painting on plaques is that several attempts may be made and the best one selected for the cake.

Mark the position for the frill around the side of the cake, taking note of the drape at the front for the flower spray. Apply the sugarpaste frill and neaten the edge with a piped design.

Attach the plaque to the cake with royal icing. Use the scriber to mark the inscription, then pipe it using a no. 1 tube and royal icing. Pipe a picot edge on the cake around the plaque using a no. 0 tube.

Mark the ribbon insertion and thread in the cut pieces of ribbon. Position the leaves and flowers on the cake, securing them with a little royal icing. Add small bows of ribbon to complete the decoration.

PROFESSIONAL TIP

When adding the finishing touches to a plaque on a cake, note that piping an edge on the plaque will exaggerate any error in the shape. So pipe the edge on the surface of the cake instead.

MARZIPAN COATING

◆

To estimate the quantity of marzipan required to cover a cake, first weigh the cake base. The weight of the cake represents the combined weight of marzipan and sugarpaste. Divide the weight in half to calculate the quantities of marzipan and sugarpaste. For example, if the cake weighs 1.8 kg (3¾ lb), you will require 900 g (1lb 14 oz) each of marzipan and sugarpaste. This calculation does not allow for coating the board.

Prepare the cake before beginning to roll out the marzipan. Trim the top of the cake with a sharp serrated knife to make it level.

PROFESSIONAL TIPS

Alcohol is used to adhere sugarpaste to marzipan as it helps to sterilize the surface. Cooled boiled water can be used instead. Also, clear alcohol will not stain the sugarpaste.

◆

On square or shaped cakes, the marzipan should be smoothed in place on the corners before working on the sides.

◆

To coat the board or a plaque, first dampen it with stock syrup. Roll out the sugarpaste to about 1 cm (½ inch) thick. Lift over the board, smoothing out any air bubbles, and trim to size. Smooth the edge by gently rubbing it with your hand or a smoother. Leave to dry.

1 Place the cake on a thin cake board cut to its exact size. Pack any uneven areas or holes in the cake with marzipan. Place the cake on a clean piece of greaseproof paper so that it may be moved easily.

4 Smooth the side of the marzipan into place with the palm of your hand. If pleats form, gently lift the marzipan slightly away from the cake, then tuck your hand down firmly into the base of the cake and smooth the paste upwards.

2 Use good quality marzipan at room temperature and knead it until it is pliable on a clean work surface. Spread a thin layer of apricot jam over the cake. Lightly dust the work surface with icing sugar, then roll out the marzipan to 1 cm (½ inch) thick.

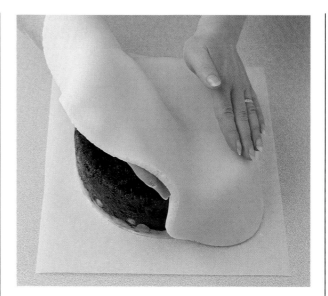

3 Check the size of the marzipan against the dimensions of the cake. Using the hands and forearms, lift the marzipan over the cake. Polish the top with a smoother to remove air bubbles.

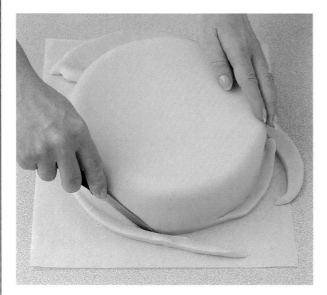

5 Trim the marzipan to about 3 cm (1¼ inch) larger than required. Use a knife to tuck the marzipan into the board around the base of the cake, then trim off the excess to ensure a neat bottom edge.

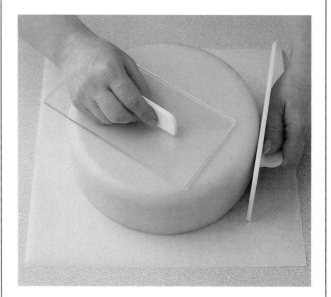

6 Using smoothers, polish the marzipan until it is completely even. Any flaws in the surface of a marzipan coating will show through the sugarpaste covering. Leave the cake to dry on the paper.

SUGARPASTE COATING

1 To colour sugarpaste, first colour a small piece of paste brighter than required, then gradually knead this into the bulk of the paste on a clean work surface. Cut the sugarpaste in half to check that the colour is even and to avoid streaks or spots.

2 Dampen the marzipan with alcohol. Roll out the sugarpaste on icing sugar to 1 cm (½ inch) thick. Using the hands and forearms, lift the paste over the cake.

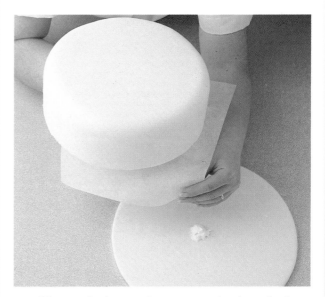

3 Polish the top with a smoother to remove air bubbles. Smooth the sides, trim off excess paste, then polish to a smooth surface. Coat the board with sugarpaste, see Professional Tips page 10.

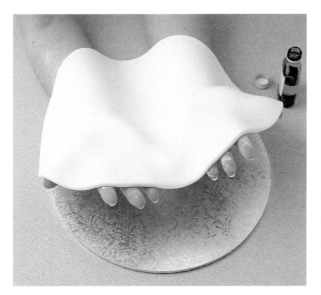

4 Place a little royal icing on the board, then remove the cake from the greaseproof paper and position it on the board. This method ensures that the cake has a neat base and the board is attractive when the cake is cut.

PLAQUE
TEMPLATE

Joy
to the
World

DESIGN ON
PLAQUE

ROSE PETALS

LEAVES

LUCY

INGREDIENTS

◆

500 g (1 lb) Royal Icing, see page 139
selection of food colours
25 × 20 cm (10 × 8 inch) oval Rich
Fruit Cake, see page 138
apricot jam, boiled and sieved
1.25 kg (2½ lb) marzipan
clear alcohol (gin or vodka)
1.25 kg (2½ lb) sugarpaste
12 Cut-out Blossom Sprays,
see page 136
12 Cut-out Blue Daphne,
see page 119
8 Roses, see page 128
200 pieces Lace, see page 46
icing (confectioner's) sugar for
rolling out

EQUIPMENT

◆

wax paper
scriber
fine paint brushes
greaseproof (parchment) paper
rolling pin
smoothers
33 × 28 cm (13 × 11 inch) oval board
dividers
scalpel
2 metres (2¼ yards) ribbon, 2 mm
(⅛ inch) wide
no. 2, 1, 0 and 00 piping tubes (tips)

ORDER OF WORK

◆

Using the template, run-out a round plaque and leave it to dry under a lamp. Scribe the picture on the plaque, then paint it with food colour.

Cover the cake with marzipan and sugarpaste. Position the template on the fresh sugarpaste coating. Cut out and remove the sugarpaste, then place the plaque in position. Neaten the edge of the sugarpaste around the plaque by smoothing it with your fingertips. Leave the coating to dry for 3 days.

Mark the ribbon insertion around the plaque and thread in the cut pieces of ribbon. Add the small sprays of flowers and ribbon loops, securing them with a small amount of sugarpaste.

Scribe the extension work and embroidery design on the side of the cake. Using a no. 0 tube, pipe the embroidery between the ribbon insertion and on the side of the cake. Use fresh icing to pipe the tiered extension work. Be sure to mix enough icing to complete all the extension work on the cake as any variation in colour will show.

Pipe the lace, inscription and butterfly wings on wax paper and leave to dry overnight. Place the wings in position and pipe the body of the butterfly on the cake, then support the wings with folded paper until the body is dry. Attach the lace and inscription with small dots of icing.

COUNTER-SUNK RUN-OUT PLAQUE

◆

When making a run-out plaque, draw several outlines of the template used so that a number of plaques may be prepared. When dry, select the best plaque for use on the cake; others may be stored in a dry place for future use.

The icing must be of the right consistency for piping the run-out. Thin the icing with egg white or water, then check the consistency. Draw a knife through the icing, then count to ten: the icing should find its own level by the count of ten. Add more royal icing if the consistency is too soft or more egg white or water if it is too stiff.

Many different plaque shapes can be used for this counter-sunk technique; for example bells, ovals and Christmas baubles all make attractive designs.

The edge of the counter-sunk plaque can be decorated with embroidery, lace, brush embroidery or ribbon to create a frame.

PROFESSIONAL TIPS

Use an arm rest when working on a freshly coated cake to help prevent accidental damage.

◆

Do not dampen the marzipan where the plaque will be positioned as this makes the sugarpaste difficult to remove.

◆

Follow the instructions for marking the ribbon insertion around the plaque, then any slight discrepancy will be at the centre top, which will be covered with flowers or a ribbon bow.

1 Secure the template on a firm flat surface and cover with wax paper. Using a no. 1 tube and fresh royal icing, outline the edge of the circle. Flood in the plaque with run-out icing. Leave to dry, then remove from paper. Scribe and paint the design.

4 Remove the cut circle of sugarpaste which should lift away easily if the marzipan underneath has not been dampened with the alcohol.

2 Place a cardboard template on the marzipan, then scribe around it. Dampen the marzipan with alcohol, taking care not to dampen the area for the plaque. Mark the plaque position on the grease-proof so that the dry patch can be located.

3 Coat the cake with sugarpaste. Position the cardboard template on the freshly coated cake, in line with the mark on the greaseproof. Using a scalpel, cut around the template, take care not to mark the rest of the cake.

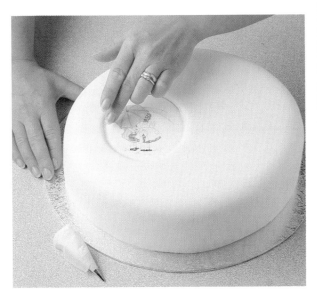

5 Position the painted plaque on the prepared cake. Gently run your fingertips around the cut edge of the sugarpaste to smooth it up to the plaque. Leave the cake to dry for 3 days before adding any further decoration.

6 Pipe royal icing between the plaque and sugar-paste to fill any gaps, then smooth the icing with your fingertip.

RIBBON INSERTION

1 Set the dividers to the required length and carefully mark the sugarpaste. Start at the bottom edge of the plaque, mark half way (work to your left), re-position the dividers at the bottom edge and mark the other side (work to your right).

2 Cut the ribbon 2.5 mm (⅛ inch) longer than the marks. Use sharp scissors to prevent the ribbon fraying. Use a scalpel to cut small slits in the sugarpaste. Hold one end of the ribbon, then insert the other end into a cut in the sugarpaste.

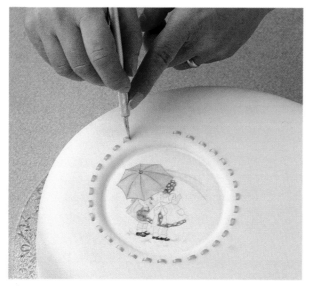

3 Gently bend the ribbon with the scalpel and tuck the second end into the next cut. Do not use ribbon with frayed ends as this will make untidy holes in the sugarpaste.

4 Small dots or flowers may be piped between the ribbon pieces to give the effect of broderie anglaise. If the cuts show slightly after the ribbon has been inserted, fill them with a little royal icing.

Lucy

PLAQUE TEMPLATE
AND DESIGN

BUTTERFLY
WINGS

LACE PIECES

EMBROIDERY DESIGN

KATIE

INGREDIENTS

◆

25 × 20 cm (10 × 8 inch) oval Rich Fruit Cake, see page 138
apricot jam, boiled and sieved
1.25 kg (2½ lb) marzipan
clear alcohol (gin or vodka)
1.75 kg (3½ lb) sugarpaste
500 g (1 lb) Royal Icing, see page 139
selection of food colours
160 pieces Lace, see page 46
16 Roses, see page 128
6 Cut-out Blossom, see page 119
25 Ribbon Loops, see page 40
icing (confectioner's) sugar for rolling out

EQUIPMENT

◆

greaseproof (parchment) paper
rolling pin
smoothers
33 × 28 cm (13 × 11 inch) oval board
thin cardboard
small sharp knife
scalpel
scriber
fine paint brushes
no. 2, 1, 0, and 00 piping tubes (tips)
1.25 metres (1½ yards) ribbon to trim board

ORDER OF WORK

◆

Cover the cake with marzipan and sugarpaste to create the counter-sunk top effect. Secure the cake on a sugarpaste-coated board using a little royal icing.

Using the template, scribe the picture on the cake, then paint the design with food colour. Pipe the inscription with chestnut-coloured royal icing.

Pipe the side embroidery and a small shell border around the base of the cake with a no. 0 tube.

Use fresh white royal icing to pipe the bridge and extension work before attaching the delicate heart-shaped lace pieces.

Finally assemble the sprays of flowers and edible ribbon loops on the cake, securing them in a small piece of sugarpaste. Add the lace pieces used to complete the top edge and trim the board with ribbon.

COUNTER-SUNK TOP

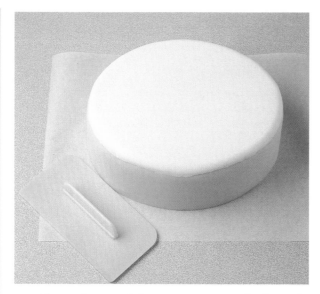

1 Cover the top of the marzipan-coated cake with white sugarpaste. Use a smoother to create a neat curved edge, then allow coating to dry. Cut an oval template from thin cardboard.

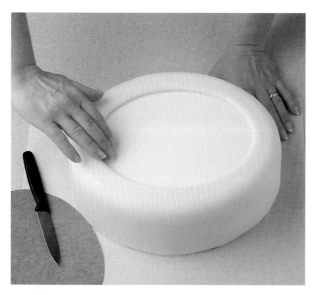

3 To neaten the cut edge of the sugarpaste, gently rub the tips of your fingers around the top. Trim off excess sugarpaste with a scalpel to help to keep a neat edge. Allow to dry.

2 Moisten only the side of the cake with alcohol, then coat it with sugarpaste. Place the oval template on the freshly coated cake and use a sharp knife to cut through the top layer of sugarpaste. The section of sugarpaste can be lifted out easily (this unwanted paste can be kneaded and reused).

PROFESSIONAL TIPS

Match ribbon, food colours and icing before starting the work.

◆

Cut a template from thin but firm cardboard which will help to prevent any damage to the surrounding sugarpaste coating.

◆

To help to prevent the edges from being uneven or jagged, use a small sharp knife to cut the sugarpaste.

◆

Never allow wires from flowers to penetrate the sugarpaste coating on a cake. The spray of flowers should be removed in one piece before the cake is cut.

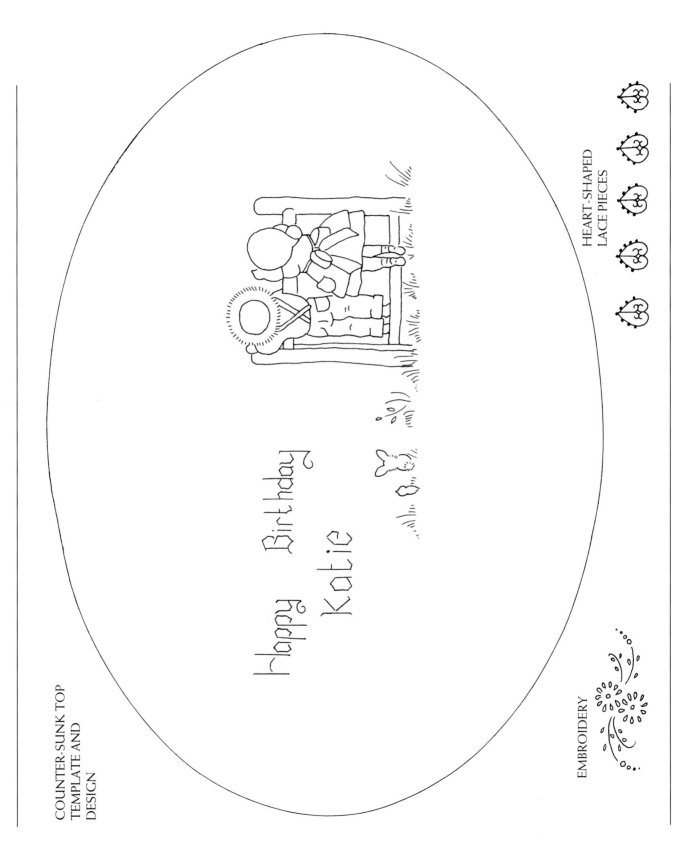

COUNTER-SUNK TOP
TEMPLATE AND
DESIGN

Happy Birthday
Katie

HEART-SHAPED
LACE PIECES

EMBROIDERY

CHRISTMAS PLAQUE

INGREDIENTS

◆

500 g (1 lb) Royal Icing, see page 139
selection of food colours

EQUIPMENT

◆

piece of thin foam
20 cm (8 inch) round cake board
palette knife
straight edge
1 metre (1 yard) ribbon to trim board
HB pencil
greaseproof (parchment) paper
scriber
paint brushes

ORDER OF WORK

◆

Place a piece of thin foam under the cake board – this will help to prevent it moving as it is coated with royal icing. Several coats of icing have to be applied and the final one should be a thin coat of softened icing. Dry the icing under a lamp to help to obtain a smooth surface.

Clean the board edge carefully with a damp cloth. Attach the ribbon to the board edge with double-sided tape or suitable adhesive. If royal icing is used to attach ribbon to the board, it may show through when dry. Take care when selecting an adhesive as some types may soak into the ribbon.

Trace the design on a circle of greaseproof paper, then scribe it on the dry plaque. Paint the mice with food colour. To complete the plaque, pipe the berries and inscription with royal icing coloured red.

Plaques are often used for competition work to represent cake tops instead of aking a rich fruit cake, which is both time consuming and expensive. Finished plaques may also be used as table decorations or displayed in other ways.

PROFESSIONAL TIP

A flexible desk-top lamp is ideal for drying icing as the bulb of the lamp can be poised at the right angle above the work, giving just enough heat to dry the icing to a sheen.

PAINTING ON SUGAR

1 Trace the picture on a circle of greaseproof paper using an HB pencil. Carefully draw over the details on the reverse side of the paper. Place the pattern on the dry royal-icing coated plaque, and scribe the outline, without moving the paper.

2 Place a selection of food colours on the edge of a plate and dilute them to the required strength with water or clear alcohol. Paint the background colour, keep the brush almost dry and brush in one direction. Allow to dry, then paint in details.

3 **Faults** If the brush is too wet or if you work on one area for too long, the icing surface will begin to dissolve giving a matt finish. To avoid this, touch the brush against absorbent kitchen paper to absorb excess colour before painting on the icing.

4 To achieve a fur or hair effect, paint small lines in the direction of growth (opposite). Use a selection of browns, black, orange and gold colours, and paint the lines until they begin to blend. Always paint from the root to give a delicate, wispy effect.

Greetings

CHRISTMAS
PLAQUE DESIGN

Arrows indicate direction
in which to paint small
lines to achieve fur effect

YOUR ENGAGEMENT

INGREDIENTS

◆

30 × 25 cm (12 × 10 inch) oval Rich Fruit Cake, see page 138
apricot jam, boiled and sieved
1.75 kg (3½ lb) marzipan
clear alcohol (gin or vodka)
2.25 kg (4½ lb) sugarpaste
1 kg (2 lb) Royal Icing, see page 139
selection of food colours
clear piping jelly
yellow petal dust
small amount of Flower Paste, see page 140
9 Open Roses, see page 126
85 pieces Lace, see page 46
12 pairs Butterfly Wings, see page 34

EQUIPMENT

◆

38 × 33 cm (15 × 13 inch) oval board
greaseproof (parchment) paper
wax paper
fine paint brushes
scriber
no. 2, 1, 0, and 00 piping tubes (tips)
ball tool
cake tilter
1.25 metres (1½ yards) ribbon, 2 mm (⅛ inch) wide for cake; 1.5 metres (1¾ yards) ribbon, 5 mm (¼ inch) wide to trim board

ORDER OF WORK

◆

Cover the cake and board with marzipan and sugarpaste, then leave to dry. Using the design, trace and run-out the mice on wax paper. When dry, remove the run-outs from the paper and paint the fur effect with food colours.

Trace the flower design and inscription, then scribe them on the cake. Paint the leaves and stems using a selection of greens, golds and browns to give natural tones and to create an impression of dimension. Use royal icing and the brush embroidery technique for the roses and leaves. When the icing has dried, dust the flower centres with yellow petal dust before piping the stamens.

Position the run-out mice on the cake and secure them with softened royal icing. Cut out some rose petals from flower paste, then smooth and gently frill their edges with a ball tool. Position the supple petals around the mouse, curling back their edges to create the effect of the mouse sitting inside the rose. Lastly, arrange the moulded roses on the cake and secure them with royal icing. Pipe the inscription using a no. 0 tube and pink royal icing. Scribe a straight line around the side of the cake 3.5 cm (1½ inch) from the board. Secure the narrow ribbon to this line with royal icing.

Use a paper pattern to mark the division for the bridge work. Use a no. 0 tube to pipe a small shell border around the cake base. Use fresh royal icing to pipe the bridge and diagonal extension work. Complete the cake side with embroidery, lace pieces and butterfly wings. Trim the board with ribbon.

BRIDGE WORK

◆

When planning the cake design, remember that long extension lines are more difficult to pipe without breaking. Cut a piece of greaseproof paper the same length and depth as the circumference and height of the cake. Fold the paper into the required number of sections. Unfold the paper and design the first section.

PROFESSIONAL TIPS

Use bridal icing sugar to make royal icing for fine piping using small tubes – it is more expensive but it is less likely to block the tubes.

◆

Use small piping bags and change the icing frequently to avoid breaks in piped lines.

◆

Tilt the cake away from you when piping bridge work; towards you when piping extension work. Work with the cake at eye level.

◆

When piping extension work, the consistency of the icing is critical: if the icing is too soft, the piped loop will break; too stiff and the icing is difficult to pipe.

◆

I find that royal icing made with fresh egg white has a better consistency for piping extension work.

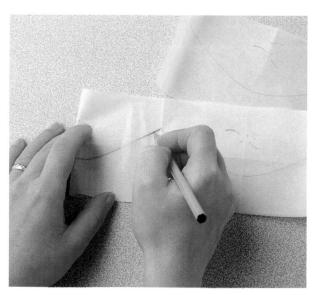

1 Draw the scalloped edge for the extension work. Divide the bottom edge of the pattern into equal sections about 3 cm (1¼ inch) long for the bridge work. Trace the design on the other sections, make sure the pencil marks only one side of the paper.

4 Build out the bridge using a no. 1 tube, adding a further three layers of loops. Allow each layer to dry to prevent sagging or breaking. Pipe each layer directly on the one below to create an even bridge. Pipe a further three layers using a no. 0 tube.

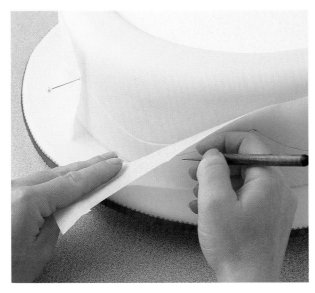

2 Fix the pattern around the cake, pencil marks out (black lines are hard to hide) and scribe through the paper, marking a line for the top edge and dots for the bridge work divisions. Use a no. 0 tube to pipe a small shell border around the bottom.

3 Tilt the cake away from you. Using fresh royal icing and a no. 2 tube, pipe a loop between two dot marks. The loop must lie flat against the side of the cake and it must not touch the board. Use a damp brush to touch the icing into place.

5 **Shaped Bridge Work** Using a no. 2 tube, pipe a loop between two dots, then dry. Continue with a no. 1 tube. Build out the bridge work, piping loops on the previous layer. Pipe each loop slightly shorter. Pipe a line around each edge.

6 When the bridge work is complete, icing of run-out consistency can be painted on the loops to neaten and strengthen the bridge. Attractive effects can be achieved by painting with coloured icing or by adding petal dust to the dry edge.

EXTENSION WORK

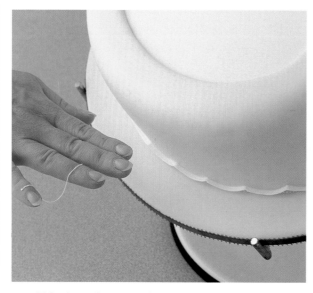

1 Tilt the cake towards you to prevent the piped thread from sagging. Pipe a thread of icing between two parted fingers, then try moving your fingers slightly. It should be possible to gently move your fingers without breaking the thread of icing.

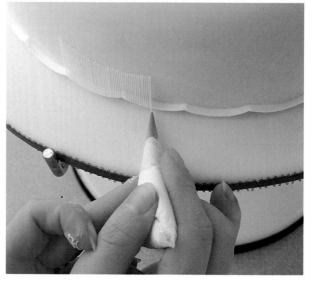

2 Using a no. 0 or 00 tube, pipe a straight line from the cake to just below the bridge work, carefully tuck the tube under the bridge to make a neat finished edge. Pipe the next line close to the first: the space should be the same width as a line of piping.

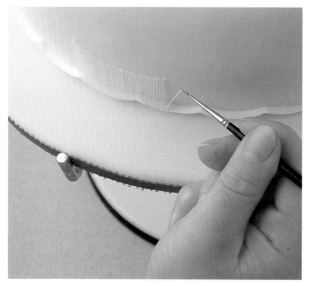

3 If the extension lines break, use a damp brush to remove them and encourage the lines to fall away from the remaining extension work. Pipe the lines straight; remove any slanting lines. Change the icing and bag frequently to prevent bursting.

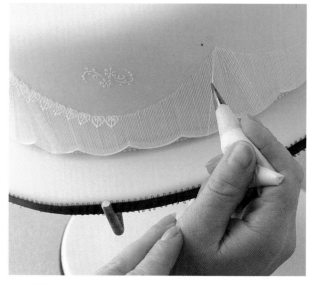

4 When over-piping extension work, pipe a further two rows of bridge work with a no. 0 tube. Tilt the cake diagonally. Pipe the curtain threads on the right-hand side; dry. Tilt the cake the opposite way; pipe curtain threads on the left side.

CURTAIN EXTENSION WORK

Complete the first layer of extension work, then use a no. 0 tube to build out the bridge work with a further two rows of icing. Tilt the cake until the overpiped curtain lines can be piped straight. Allow the left side of the curtain work to dry, then tilt the cake to the right and pipe the remaining strands.

DIAGONAL EXTENSION WORK

A tilting turntable is an asset for working this design. The cake must be positioned at an angle such that the extension lines are piped vertically (straight). When the first layer of extension lines have dried, build out the bridge work with a further two rows of icing using a no. 0 tube. Tilt the cake in the opposite direction and overpipe five diagonal lines to each scallop of bridge work.

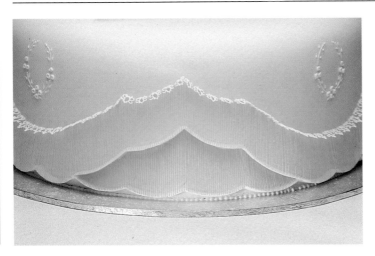

TIERED EXTENSION WORK

Scribe the design on the cake and pipe the bridge work. Pipe the deeper orange extension lines using a no. 0 or 00 tube and allow to dry. Pipe a second bridge above the extension work using the same tubes and technique for the first bridge, then use a damp brush to smooth each layer into the lower bridge where they join. Paint with icing of run-out consistency and allow to dry. Next, pipe the second row of extension work and decorate the top edge with lace pieces.

MOUSE RUN-OUT
TEMPLATE

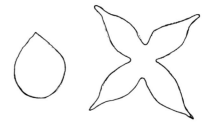

FUCHSIA CUTTER TEMPLATES

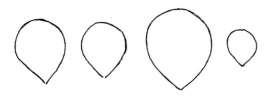

ROSE PETAL TEMPLATES

PRIMROSE
CUTTER TEMPLATE

DAPHNE
CUTTER TEMPLATE

BUTTERFLY WINGS

BLOSSOM CUTTER
TEMPLATES

BLUEBELL CUTTER
TEMPLATE

EMBROIDERY

LACE PIECES

FLOWER DESIGN

ON YOUR
ENGAGEMENT

MOUSE
RUN-OUT
TEMPLATE

FUCHSIA GALA

INGREDIENTS

◆

46 × 28 cm (18 × 11 inch), 33 ×
46 cm (13 × 18 inch) and 23 × 13 cm
(9 × 5 inch) diamond-shaped Rich
Fruit Cakes, see page 138
apricot jam, boiled and sieved
4 kg (8 lb) marzipan
Edible Ribbon pieces: bottom tier 70,
middle tier 50, top tier 30, see page 52
confectioner's varnish
clear alcohol (gin or vodka)
4.75 kg (9½ lb) sugarpaste
1 kg (2 lb) Royal Icing, see page 139
Cut-out Blossom: bottom tier 30,
middle tier 30, see page 119
Fuchsia Sprays: bottom tier 10,
middle tier 8, top tier 6, see
pages 124/136
Edible Ribbon Loops: bottom tier 30,
middle tier 24, top tier 18, see page
52
500 g (1 lb) Flower Paste, see page 140

cornflour (cornstarch) for rolling out
white vegetable fat for rolling out
egg white

EQUIPMENT

◆

66 × 38 cm (26 × 15 inch), 48 × 28 cm
(19 × 11 inch) and 35 × 20 cm (14 × 8
inch) diamond-shaped cake
boards • rolling pin • ruler
wooden dowels: 4 each 19 cm (7½
inch) and 18 cm (7 inch) plus extra
8.25 metres (9 yards) each of thin
pink and white cord
greaseproof (parchment) paper
no. 1 and 0 piping tubes (tips)
scriber
garrett frill cutter
cocktail stick (toothpick)
scalpel
hooked modelling tool
bunch of dried gypsophila

ORDER OF WORK

◆

Cover the cakes with marzipan. Prepare the edible ribbon pieces, leave to dry and paint with confectioner's varnish. Then remove from the wooden dowel. Cover the cakes with sugarpaste. Position the template on the fresh sugarpaste coating and insert the prepared edible ribbon pieces. Leave the coating to dry.

Use a no. 1 tube to pipe a small shell border around the base of the cake. Use a greaseproof paper pattern to mark the position of the frill on the side of the cake, taking note of the drape at the front for the flower spray. Apply the sugarpaste frill. Use a no. 0 tube and white royal icing to pipe the embroidery between the ribbon insertion and on the top of the frill.

Mark the position for the pillars on the bottom and middle tiers, then insert the dowels through the cake. Make a pencil mark on each dowel level with the top of the cake. Remove one piece of dowel at a time and cover the top end (exposed area) with pink and white cord in a candy striped pattern, then replace it. By marking each dowel individually, the decoration will be level with the cake. Add cut-out blossom to the base of the pillars. Complete the cakes with sprays of flowers and edible ribbon loops.

GARRETT FRILL

◆

Thinly rolled sugarpaste makes a delicate frill which appears to be cut in one strip but it is cleverly joined by folding the cut edge to look like a pleat.

1 Scribe the frill design on the cake. Roll out the sugarpaste thinly on a dusting of cornflour and use a cutter to cut out the frill. Lay the cocktail stick on the edge of the sugarpaste and gently roll it to frill the edge of the paste.

PROFESSIONAL TIPS

If the sugarpaste is too thick the cocktail stick will not roll, instead it will cut into the frill.

◆

If the sugarpaste is too soft or sticky, a small amount of flower paste can be kneaded into it to strengthen it.

◆

Roll out only enough paste for cutting one or two lengths of frill at a time as the paste dries quickly.

◆

Put some cornflour into a new piece of stocking and tie the top to make a cornflour bag which may be used to lightly dust surfaces.

4 Pleat the frill at the top of the scallop design to make a neat point. To join on the second frill, cut through the paste (do not shape the end) and fold back the cut end before introducing it to the cake. The cut edge will look like a pleat.

2 Dampen the scribed line on the side of the cake with water. To create the drape at the front of the cake, taper one side of the frill with a sharp knife.

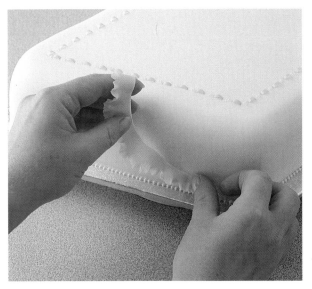

3 Slide the frill over your left hand, then introduce it into position. Hold your left hand high when the frill is being attached to an upward curve of the scallop. Lower your hand when working on a downward curve. This prevents the paste tearing.

5 While the sugarpaste is supple, carefully lift the frill with a soft dry brush to make it stand away from the cake. A second layer of frills can be added.

6 Trim the top edge of the frill with a scalpel and remove the excess cuttings with a hooked modelling tool. Take care not to cut too much of the sugarpaste as this could cause the frill to come away from the side of the cake.

EDIBLE RIBBON LOOPS AND BOWS

1 Roll out the flowerpaste as thinly as possible on a lightly greased board. Cut the paste into 2.5 mm (⅛ inch) wide strips. Take care to cut the strips accurately and keep the paste covered with polythene as you shape the loops to prevent it drying out.

2 Cut each strip of paste to the required length. Hold the two ends between your index fingers and gently roll them together. Leave the loops to dry before painting with confectioner's varnish to give them a satin sheen. Bows, below left, should also be painted with confectioner's varnish when dry.

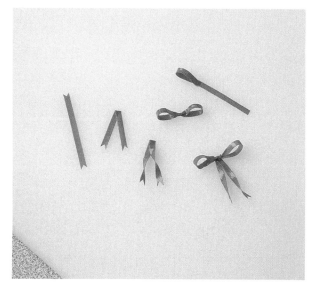

3 To make a bow, cut a piece of flower paste 2.5 mm (⅛ inch) wide. Cut the ends into 'V' shapes, then fold the paste in half and twist each piece slightly. Fold a second strip of paste, both ends to the middle; attach this to ribbon tail with egg white.

EMBROIDERY DESIGN
TEMPLATE

FUCHSIA CUTTER
TEMPLATE

DIAMOND TOP DECORATION

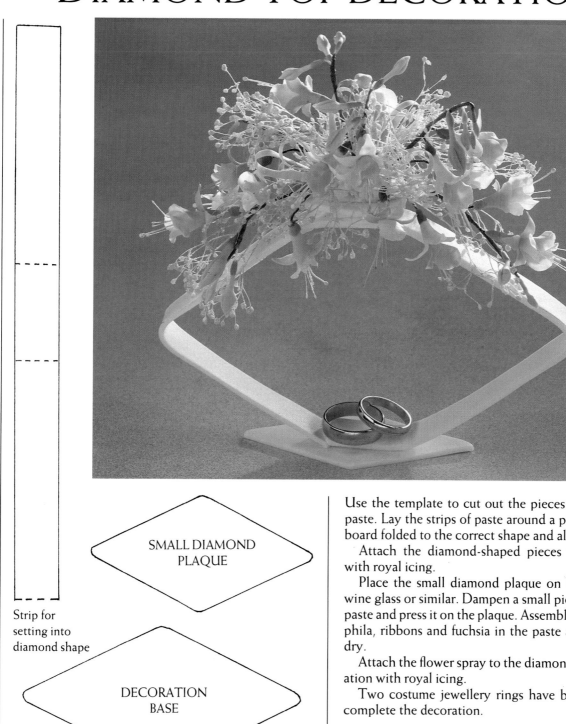

Strip for
setting into
diamond shape

SMALL DIAMOND
PLAQUE

DECORATION
BASE

Use the template to cut out the pieces from flower paste. Lay the strips of paste around a piece of cardboard folded to the correct shape and allow to dry.

Attach the diamond-shaped pieces to the base with royal icing.

Place the small diamond plaque on an upturned wine glass or similar. Dampen a small piece of sugarpaste and press it on the plaque. Assemble the gypsophila, ribbons and fuchsia in the paste and leave to dry.

Attach the flower spray to the diamond top decoration with royal icing.

Two costume jewellery rings have been used to complete the decoration.

Note: Do not arrange the flowers in position on the stand as any pressure will break the base.

THE SHEEP DOG

INGREDIENTS

◆

25 × 20 cm (10 × 8 inch) oval Rich
Fruit Cake, see page 138
apricot jam, boiled and sieved
1.25 kg (2½ lb) marzipan
clear alcohol (gin and vodka)
1.5 kg (3 lb) sugarpaste
500 g (1 lb) Royal Icing, see page 139
selection of food colours
60 Cut-out Blossom (small and
medium), see page 119
120 pieces Lace, see page 46

EQUIPMENT

◆

33 × 28 cm (13 × 11 inch) oval board
wax paper
paint brushes
pair of compasses
thin cardboard
no. 1, 0 and 00 piping tubes (tips)
scriber
greaseproof (parchment) paper
corrugated cardboard
tilting turntable
1.25 metres (1½ yards) ribbon to trim
board

ORDER OF WORK

◆

Cover the cake with marzipan and sugarpaste. Cover the board with sugarpaste. Leave to dry. Run-out the figures on wax paper and leave to dry. Remove from the paper and paint the details with food colour.

Cut a petal-shaped template from thin cardboard to fit the cake top. Place the template on the cake. Using a no. 0 tube, pipe a picot edge around the template.

Scribe the picture of the sheep dog on the cake and paint it with food colour. Place the run-out figures in position. Secure the figures and the cut-out blossom to the cake with royal icing.

Use a greaseproof paper pattern to scribe the side designs on the cake, then paint the rabbits and kittens with food colour. Using a no. 0 tube, pipe a small shell border around the cake base. Prepare the extension loops and attach them to the cake, then pipe the extension strands using a no. 00 tube. Attach the lace pieces and trim the board edge with ribbon.

PROFESSIONAL TIPS

Use your fingertips to attach the lace to the cake. I find tweezers difficult to control.

◆

Take care to ensure that all the lace is positioned at the same angle from the cake.

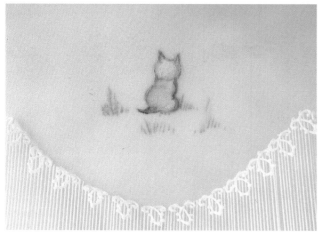

LINE-SUPPORTED EXTENSION WORK

◆

Ribbon or flowers may be arranged and attached to the bottom edge of the cake before the bridges are set in place. The decoration around the edge shows through the finished work and looks most attractive.

1 Draw an oval the size of the coated cake, then divide it into 10 sections. Use a set of compasses to draw the scallop on one section, then trace it on the other sections for accuracy. Trace the scallop several times to make the bridge pattern.

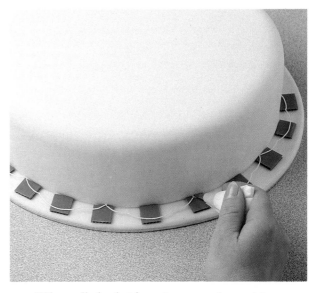

4 When all the bridge pieces are in position, secure them to the cake with dots of royal icing.

SIDE DESIGN

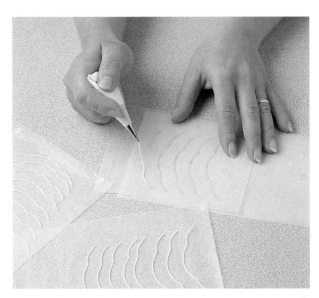

2 Cover the bridge pattern with wax paper. Use a no. 1 tube to pipe the bridge (scallop). Care must be taken to pipe the bridge pieces accurately. Leave to dry flat.

3 Place 2 small squares of 2.5 mm (⅛ inch) thick corrugated card on the cake board under the position of each bridge. The card must be of the right thickness to space the bridge from the cake board. Support the bridge pieces in place on the card.

5 Tilt the cake towards you. Using a no. 0 or 00 tube, pipe the extension lines from the cake to under the bridge work. Do not allow the tube to hit the bridge work as the icing will break.

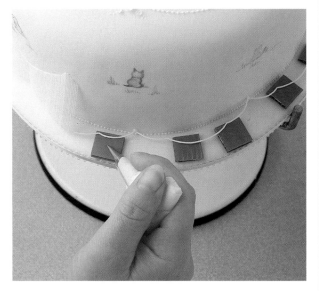

6 As the extension work is piped, carefully remove the pieces of card. Corrugated card is very useful as it can be compressed, making it easy to remove from the board without damaging the extension work.

LACE

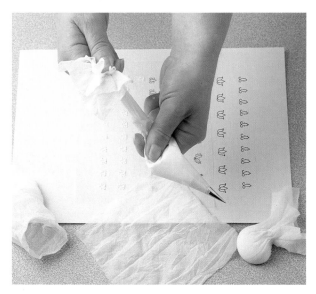

1 Place a spoonful of icing on a piece of new stocking fabric and gather up the fabric edges. Place the icing in the piping bag and grip the neck of the bag, then pull out the fabric. The icing will be strained into the bag, without large sugar crystals.

2 Cover the lace pattern with wax tissue paper. Use a no. 0 or 00 tube to pipe the lace, then neaten any joins with a damp brush. Allow to dry. Remove the lace by placing your finger under the tissue, then slide a thin knife under the lace piece.

3 Pipe two small dots of royal icing on the cake. Hold a piece of lace gently between your index finger and thumb, then slide it down the cake to the piped dots.

4 Tilt the lace into position. This method helps to keep the icing underneath the lace, giving a neat edge.

TEMPLATES FOR
RUN-OUT FIGURES

SHEEP DOG TEMPLATE

TEMPLATES FOR
LACE PIECES

SHEEP DOG DESIGN

BALLERINA

MAIN SKILLS

Edible Ribbon Insertion
Run-out Figure

◆

ADDITIONAL SKILLS

Marzipan Coating,
see page 10
Sugarpaste Coating,
see page 12
Painting on Sugar,
see page 26
Roses, see page 128
Cut-out Blossom,
see page 119
Double Bridgeless Extension Work,
see page 110
Lace, see page 46

◆

Design and Templates, see page 53

INGREDIENTS

◆

small amount of Flower Paste, see page 140
confectioner's varnish
23 cm (9 inch) round Rich Fruit Cake, see page 138
apricot jam, boiled and sieved
1.25 kg (2½ lb) marzipan
clear alcohol (gin or vodka)
1.5 kg (3 lb) sugarpaste
about 500 g (1 lb) Royal Icing, see page 139
4 miniature Roses, see page 128
12 Cut-out Blossom (small and medium), see page 119
selection of food colours
100 pieces Lace, see page 46
white vegetable fat for rolling out

EQUIPMENT

◆

rolling pin
ruler
scalpel
6 mm (¼ inch) diameter dowelling
fine paint brushes
30 cm (12 inch) round cake board
fine cardboard
masking tape
wax paper
no 1, 0 and 00 piping tubes (tips)
cranked pallet knife
scriber

ORDER OF WORK

◆

Prepare the lilac-coloured edible ribbon strips. Cover the cake with marzipan.

Cover the cake with sugarpaste. Place a round template on the cake top. Gently tuck the edible ribbon pieces into the soft sugarpaste and leave the cake to dry.

Make the run-out ballerina and leave to dry. Scribe the inscription and stool on the cake. Use a no. 0 tube and pink royal icing to pipe the inscription. Paint the stool directly on the sugarpaste with food colours. Place the ballerina on the cake and secure the figure and flowers with royal icing.

Use a greaseproof paper pattern to scribe the extension work design on the side of the cake. Pipe the border around the cake edge using a no. 0 tube. Trim the board edge with ribbon and lace, placing the join at the back. Pipe the embroidery between the ribbon insertion and on the side of the cake.

Pipe the bridgeless extension work using a no. 00 tube and pink royal icing for the first layer, followed by a second layer in white royal icing. Use lilac royal icing to match the ribbon and pipe the lace pieces on wax paper: extra pieces may be required as the glycerine in the colour makes the lace more fragile. Leave to dry, then secure to the cake with dots of white royal icing.

RUN-OUT FIGURE

♦

Thin the icing with egg white or water to obtain the correct consistency for run-out figures. To check the consistency, draw a knife through the icing, then count to ten: the icing should find its own level by the count of ten. Add more royal icing if the consistency is too soft or more egg white or water if it is too stiff.

To complete the ballerina run-out, paint the hair details with a fine brush and a selection of food colours. Highlight cheeks, thighs and arms with pink powder colour, applied with a soft dry brush for a natural effect. Mix equal quantities of flower paste and sugarpaste for the tu-tu.

PROFESSIONAL TIPS

Dry each part of the run-out for a few minutes under a warm lamp to give a shiny surface.

♦

Use a no. 0 or 1 tube to pipe the run-out icing, as the small hole helps to prevent bubbles forming in the icing.

♦

Dry run-outs in a warm dry atmosphere as damp conditions may cause the icing to become chalky, resulting in a run-out which lacks gloss and breaks easily.

♦

Take care when colouring icing for run-out work as some food colours contain glycerine which will prevent the run-out drying firmly enough to be removed from the wax paper.

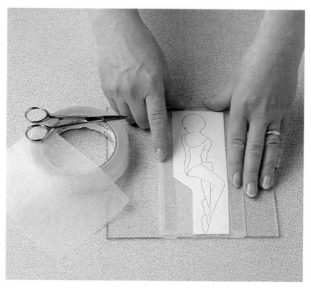

1 Secure the simplified drawing of the figure on page 53 to a rigid, flat surface. Spray adhesive is excellent for this purpose. Tape some wax paper tightly over the design. Avoid having creases in the paper. Work on two or three figures at once.

4 Use a scalpel to cut the wax paper from the board. Do not try to lift the tape off as the figures are fragile. Then release the run-out from the paper by carefully sliding a cranked pallet knife under it.

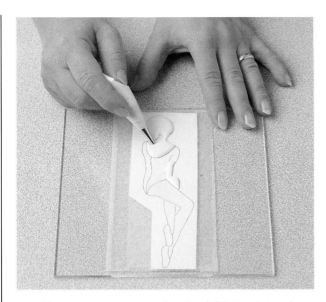

2 Using a no. 0 or 1 tube, half fill the icing bag with the icing. An outline is unnecessary when using icing of the correct consistency. First flood areas that appear furthest away. Use a brush to ease icing into all areas. Dry under a lamp.

3 Gradually build up the figure – do not work on two areas that touch as they may run together. The numbers in the illustration indicate the order of work. When the run-out is complete leave it to dry in a warm place.

5 For the tu-tu, roll out the paste as thin as possible, then cut it into 6 × 1 cm (2½ × ½ inch) strips. Frill one edge with a cocktail stick and pleat this skirt, then fasten it to the figure with egg white. Repeat several layers of frills.

6 Scribe the pattern of the stool on the cake, then paint it with food colour. Use a cranked pallet knife to lift the figure, and secure it to the cake with royal icing when it is accurately positioned.

EDIBLE RIBBON INSERTION

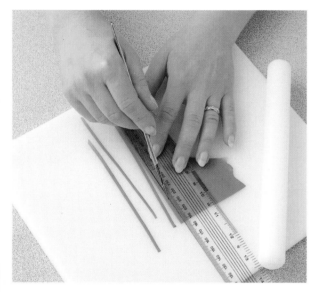

1 Roll out coloured flower paste as thin as possible on a lightly greased board. Cut 2.5 mm (⅛ inch) strips, measuring them accurately. Cut the strips into 1 cm (½ inch) long pieces – 50 are used on this cake. Cover the paste with plastic to prevent drying.

2 Grease the dowelling, then lay the paste strips over it and leave them to dry. Paint the dry ribbon pieces with confectioner's varnish and leave them to dry on the dowel.

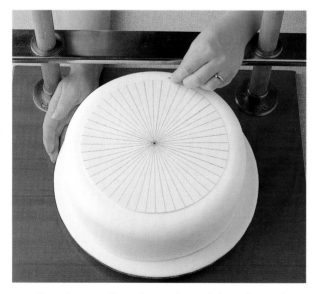

3 Divide a cardboard template of the cake surface into equal portions – the number of sections depends on the size of the cake. Place the template on the fresh sugarpaste coating, then gently push the edible ribbon pieces into the paste.

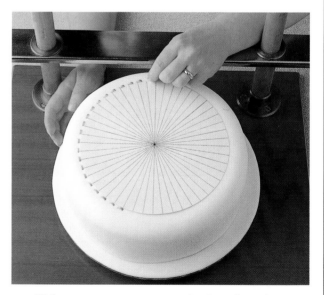

4 Take great care not to touch, disturb or damage the cake coating. When all the ribbon pieces are in position remove the template and allow the coating to dry.

BALLERINA
RUN-OUT TEMPLATE

On Your
21st
Birthday

BALLERINA
DESIGN

STOOL TEMPLATE

Numbers
show order
in which
to run-out
sections

BLACKBERRIES

INGREDIENTS

◆

25 × 20 cm (10 × 8 inch) oval Rich Fruit Cake, see page 138
apricot jam, boiled and sieved
1.25 kg (2½ lb) marzipan
1.5 kg (3 lb) Royal Icing, see page 139
selection of food colours
6 Edible Ribbon Loops, see page 40
45 Cut-out Blossom (small and medium), see page 119
2 Apple Blossom, see page 129
170 pieces Lace, see page 46
Blackberry Spray, see page 132

EQUIPMENT

◆

palette knife
straight edge or long knife
small sharp knife
.5 metres (1¾ yards) ribbon and lace to trim board
3 × 1 kg (2 lb) weights
turntable
metal side scraper
36 × 20 cm (14 × 12 inch) oval cake board
scalpel
no. 2, 1, 0 and 00 piping tubes (tips)
greaseproof (parchment) paper
scriber • fine paint brushes
wax paper

ORDER OF WORK

◆

Cover the cake with marzipan and cut out a wedge, then coat the cake and board with royal icing. Cut the icing along the wedge edge after each coat has dried. Decorate with a bow. Secure the cake to the board with a little icing. Place a cardboard template on the cake and outline its shape with a line of icing using a no. 1 tube. Neaten the wedge cut with graduated line piping, using no. 2 and 1 tubes.

Paint three leaves between each scallop on the top of the cake. Use royal icing to attach the edible ribbon and cut-out blossom in neat sprays. Make a greaseproof paper template for the side design, then outline the reverse side using an H pencil. Lightly scribe the design on the cake.

Use a no. 1 tube to pipe a shell border around the cake base before piping the bridge and extension work, using a no. 2 and 0 or 00 tubes.

Pipe the run-out mouse in white royal icing and the blanket in pink; when dry remove both from the wax paper. Use food colour to paint the tree on the cake and the details on the mouse. Secure the run-out and unwired flowers to the cake with royal icing. Secure the pink lace pieces above the extension work and around the top edge of the cake, using a no. 0 tube and white royal icing.

Lastly, position the blackberry spray on the cake, taking care not to disturb the lace pieces. Trim the board edge with ribbon and lace.

ROYAL ICING COATING

◆

The techniques described here are for cakes and dummies. Make the royal icing a day in advance. Gently stir the royal icing but do not beat it.

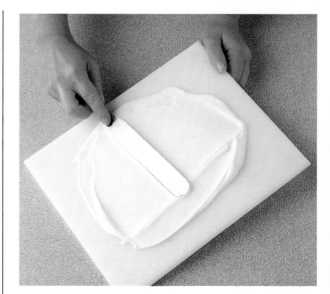

1 Place some icing on a grease-free board and work it with a palette knife to remove the large air bubbles. Place the cake on a piece of foam rubber to prevent it from slipping.

LACE PIECES

PROFESSIONAL TIPS

Use bridal icing sugar for the final coat, as the small sugar particles will help to give a smooth surface.

◆

The final coat of icing should be thinned with softened icing.

◆

Do not coat the cake on the board, as the side scraper will catch on the paper and prevent the coating from being perfect.

◆

Adding 5 ml (1 tsp) glycerine to every 500 g (1 lb) royal icing produces a softer texture to the coating.

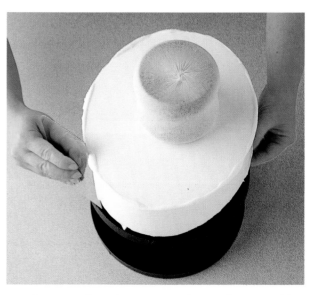

4 Position the cake on a weight on the turntable. Place another heavy weight on top of the cake. Spread the icing on the side of the cake. Hold the scraper against the cake and rotate the turntable. Remove the excess icing from the edges.

2 Spread the prepared icing on the cake top. Position the straight edge (or knife) on the far edge of the cake, then pull it across the surface. If the coating has noticeable flaws, clean the blade and draw it across the cake a second time.

3 Remove the excess icing from the side of the cake with a palette knife. Allow the icing to dry completely before continuing.

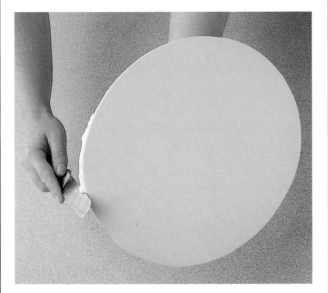

5 Place the board on a piece of foam rubber. Coat with royal icing as for the cake top and remove the excess icing from the board edge using a knife. Apply thin layers of icing to obtain a good surface.

6 When the icing is dry, remove the scraper 'take off' mark and any excess icing by gently scraping the coating with a sharp knife. Apply two or three coats of icing to the cake to achieve an even, smooth surface.

CUTTING A WEDGE

LEAF TEMPLATES

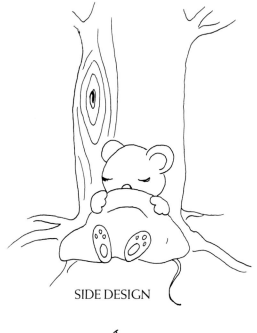

SIDE DESIGN

TOP DESIGN

1 Turn the cake upside-down on greaseproof paper. Use a set square to remove a neat wedge and cut through the cake. Turn the cake the right way up. Place the cake on a thin board cut to the same size, including the marzipan.

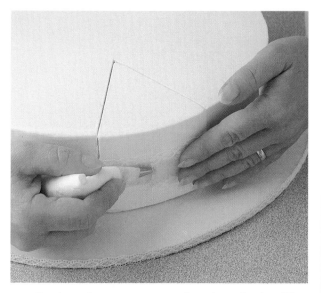

4 Replace the paper-covered wedge of cake. The greaseproof paper should not be visible. Secure the ribbon ends to the side of the cake with a little royal icing and decorate the join with a bow.

2 Coat the cake with royal icing. Use a sharp knife or scalpel and set square to cut through each layer of dry icing along the wedge. When the final coating has dried and been cut, lift out the wedge, use a knife to clean up the inside edge of the cake.

3 Cut a piece of greaseproof paper twice the depth of the marzipan-coated cake, measure it around the wedge and cut the paper 5 mm (¼ inch) smaller. Place a length of ribbon on the paper, fold the paper in half. Wrap this around the wedge.

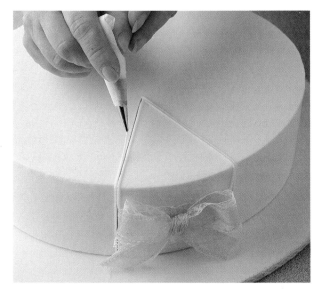

5 Use a no. 2 tube to pipe a line of icing on each side of the cut wedge, on the top and side of the cake – this will disguise the cut mark.

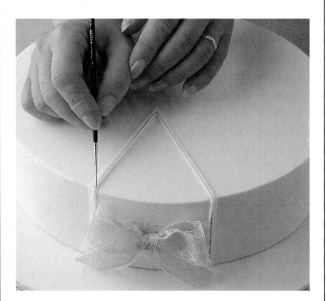

6 Use a no. 1 tube to overpipe the piped line. Pipe 2 more lines of icing: 1 on the cake and 1 on the wedge (making 4 rows of piping in total). This technique is known as *graduated line piping*.

TO YOU BOTH

INGREDIENTS

◆

20 cm (8 inch) round Rich Fruit Cake,
see page 138
apricot jam, boiled and sieved
1 kg (2 lb) marzipan
clear alcohol (gin or vodka)
1.25 kg (2½ lb) sugarpaste
selection of food colours
500 g (1 lb) Royal Icing, see page 139
small amount of Flower Paste,
see page 140
24 Violets, see page 130
21 Leaves without wires,
see page 125
6 Cut-out Blossom (small),
see page 119
2 Edible Ribbon Bows, see page 40,
plus larger moulded bow
70 pieces Lace, see page 46

EQUIPMENT

◆

30 cm (12 inch) round board
scriber
no. 1, 0 and 00 piping tubes (tips)
fine paint brushes
greaseproof (parchment) paper
1.25 metres (1½ yards) ribbon to
trim board

ORDER OF WORK

◆

Coat the cake with marzipan and cream-coloured sugarpaste. Coat the board with sugarpaste in a deeper shade of cream. Leave to dry. Position the cake on the board.

The cake has to be turned upside down to pipe some of the bridge loops for this advanced extension work. Scribe the extension work design on the side of the cake. Pipe a small shell edge around the base of the cake using a no. 0 tube. Use fresh white royal icing to pipe the bridge loops (no. 0 tube) on pins and the extension work (no. 00 tube).

Using a no. 1 tube, run-out the boy and the face and legs for the girl, then leave to dry under a lamp. Paint the details on the figures with food colour. Make the girl's dress with flower paste, using the bas relief method. Secure the run-outs to the cake with royal icing. Trace the pattern and use to scribe the inscription on the cake. Then use a no. 0 tube and violet-coloured royal icing to pipe the inscription.

Assemble the sprays of violets and leaves into small pieces of sugarpaste on the cake, taking care not to disturb the extension work. Add the cut-out blossom and bows to the run-out figures. Finally, complete the side of the cake by adding the lace pieces. Trim the board with ribbon.

CREATING DIMENSION IN DESIGN

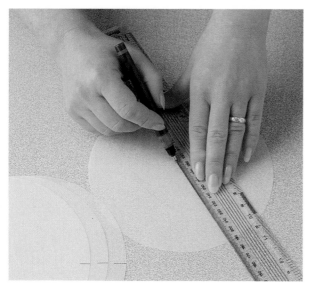

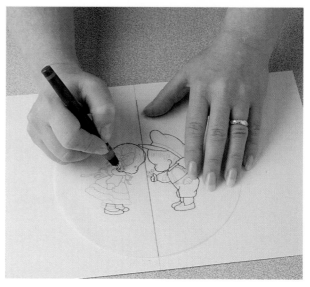

1 Cut-out 4 greaseproof paper circles the size of the cake. Draw a line across the diameter of the first circle, mark the top and bottom of the diameter on the other circles. These diameter marks are vital to line up the design.

2 Draw the complete design of the cake top on a sheet of cartridge paper. Mark a line through the centre of the design. Position the first greaseproof circle over the design: the diameter lines must match.

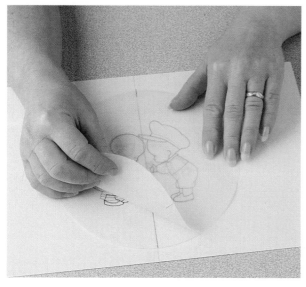

3 Draw the details for the first technique to be used, in this cake the run-out boy, the girl's face and legs.

4 Position the second greaseproof paper circle, ensuring that the diameter marks line up with the pattern below. Draw the girl's bas relief dress on this pattern. Overlay circles of paper until the complete design has been transferred to greaseproof.

FIGURE
RUN-OUTS

MOULDED BOW
AND ARMS

Note: dotted
lines should
align to build
up design

BAS-RELIEF
DRESS

COMPLETE
DESIGN

*Congratulations
to you both*

CONGRATULATIONS

INGREDIENTS

❖

25 × 20 cm (10 × 8 inch) oval Rich
Fruit Cake, see page 138
apricot jam, boiled and sieved
1.25 kg (2½ lb) marzipan
clear alcohol (gin or vodka)
1.5 kg (3 lb) sugarpaste
500 g (1 lb) Royal Icing, see page 139
selection of food colours
silver snow-flake petal dust
small amount of Mexican Paste, see
page 140, mixed with an equal
quantity of sugarpaste
4 Fuchsias, see page 124
6 Bluebells, see page 34
35 Cut-out Blossom, see page 119
10 Cut-out Daphne, see page 119
3 Primroses, see page 119
6 Leaves, see page 125
4 Edible Ribbon Bows, see page 40
80 pieces Lace, see page 46
egg white for attaching decoration
icing (confectioner's) sugar for
rolling out

EQUIPMENT

❖

30 × 26 cm (12 × 10 inch) oval cake
board
1.25 metres (1½ yards) ribbon to trim
board
wax paper
scriber
no. 1, 0 and 00 piping tubes (tips)
fine paint brushes
rolling pin
scalpel
cocktail stick (toothpick)
greaseproof (parchment) paper

ORDER OF WORK

❖

Cover the cake with marzipan. Cover the cake and board with white
sugarpaste. When the coating has dried, place the cake on the board. Run-out
the bridegroom, bride's face and baby mouse, then dry. Scribe the simplified
design on the cake. Use a no. 0 tube and pink royal icing to pipe the
inscription.

Use food colours to paint the stalks and leaves, bridesmaid and veil. Paint the
details on the run-outs, then position them on the cake and secure with royal
icing. Add the bas relief of the bride. Make the wedding dress and lightly dust it
with silver snow-flake petal dust before positioning the groom's hat, the
flowers, leaves and bows. Secure the flowers to the cake with royal icing.

Mark two straight lines around the side of the cake 4 cm (1¾ inches) and 5 cm
(2 inches) from the board. Use a paper pattern to mark the divisions for the
dropped loops (piped using a no. 1 tube). Use a no. 0 tube to pipe a small dot
border around the base of the cake. Pipe the extension work using a no. 00 tube
and white royal icing. Complete the cake by adding the lace pieces.

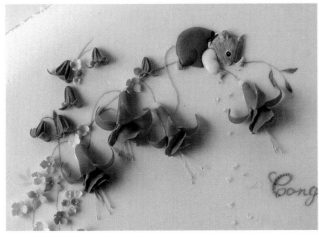

BAS RELIEF

◆

The figures are built up on the undressed outline. For the bride, added in step 3, cut a silhouette of the bride's body from the prepared Mexican and sugarpaste mixture. This should be about 2.5 mm (⅛ inch) smaller than the finished design. Once the petticoat frill is in place, continue to build out the bride's dress by adding layers of frilled paste.

PROFESSIONAL TIPS

To make the flowers sit flat on the cake, cut a section from the moulded fuchsia and bluebells before the paste dries.

◆

When developing bas relief figures, always begin with the naked shape and add the clothes in the order in which you would dress. For example, model the socks before the shoes and make the petticoat before the dress.

◆

Faces on bas relief figures can be moulded from paste or run-out of royal icing.

◆

A small amount of white vegetable fat can be kneaded into the paste if it dries too quickly.

1 Scribe the simplified design on the cake: it is not necessary to mark each flower. Use food colour to paint the details which appear furthest away, in this case the flowers, stalks and bridesmaid.

4 The lace design on the skirt edge is achieved by cutting small holes in the paste using the tip of a no. 0 tube. Shape a small piece of paste for the bride's arm following the template and model the top hat; leave both to dry.

2 Prepare the run-out figures. When they are completely dry remove them from the wax paper and paint in the details. Arrange the run-outs on the cake, when in position secure them with royal icing.

3 Secure the pliable silhouette of the bride using egg white. Roll out a thin strip of the same paste and frill one edge with a cocktail stick. Pleat the other edge between your fingers. Use egg white to stick this petticoat to the silhouette.

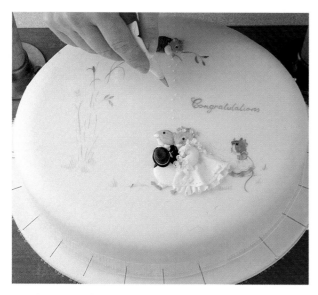

5 Position the bride's arm while the dress paste is pliable. Use a soft brush to gently ease the frills in place. When the figure is dry, brush the dress with silver snow-flake petal dust. Pipe the confetti with white icing; paint the colours when it is dry.

6 Arrange the flowers on the cake and make the bride's head dress and posy from small blossom. Secure the flowers to the cake with royal icing.

TOP DESIGN

Congratulations

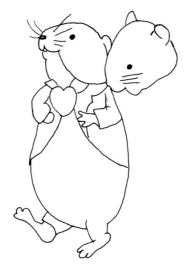

TEMPLATES
FOR MICE
RUN-OUTS

MOULDED HAT

PAINTED
BRIDESMAID
TEMPLATE

GOD BLESS MARC

MAIN SKILL

Creating Dimension –
Using an Air Brush

◆

ADDITIONAL
SKILLS

Marzipan Coating,
see page 10
Royal Icing Coating,
see page 56
Graduated Line
Piping, see page 92
Line-supported
Extension Work,
see page 44
Run-out Figures,
see page 50
Cut-out Blossom,
see page 119
Painting on Sugar,
see page 26
Lace, see page 46

◆

Design and Template,
see page 73

INGREDIENTS

◆

23 cm (9 inch) round Rich Fruit Cake,
see page 138
apricot jam, boiled and sieved
1.25 kg (2½ lb) marzipan
1.5 kg (3 lb) Royal Icing, see page
139
selection of food colours
18 Cut-out Blossom, see page 119
1 Edible Bow, see page 40
110 pieces Lace, see page 46

EQUIPMENT

◆

30 cm (12 inch) round cake board
greaseproof (parchment) paper
no 2, 1, 0 and 00 piping tubes (tips)
wax paper
air brush
scalpel
oil board (manilla board)
1.25 metres (1½ yards) ribbon to trim
board

ORDER OF WORK

◆

Coat the marzipan-covered cake and the board with royal icing. Secure
the cake to the board, with a little icing.

Make a greaseproof paper pattern for the side of the cake. The graduated
line design (using no. 2, 1 and 0 tubes) can be achieved by piping the
bottom row of loops on the cake, then turning the cake upside-down to
pipe the top row. Here, the cake stand illustrated on
page 141 has been used.

Pipe the bridge loops on wax paper and leave to dry. Secure the dry loops
to the side of the cake and pipe the extension work, using a no. 0 or 00
tube. Run-out the figure of the boy. Use white royal icing to run-out the
bear's arm and leg. Leave to dry under a lamp.

Air brush the silhouette of the bear on the cake, lightly spray the run-out
arm and leg with colour. Take care not to allow the icing to become 'wet'
with colour as this will spoil the gloss on the run-out.

Position the petal-shaped template on the cake and pipe a picot edge
using a no. 1 tube. Remove the template. Place three blossom in each
scallop, securing them to the cake with icing, then complete the little
sprays with piped leaves.

Use a fine brush and food colour to paint the details on the bear and run-
out figure. Scribe and pipe the inscription, then secure the run-outs to the
cake with icing.

Complete the decoration by adding the bow to the teddy bear and lace
around the edge of the cake. Trim the board with ribbon.

USING AN AIR BRUSH

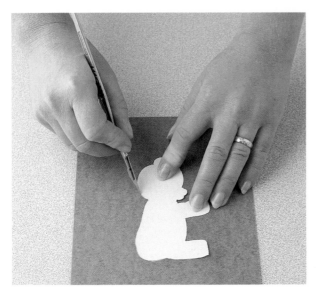

1 Trace the outline of the teddy bear on the oil board, then carefully cut out the shape using a scalpel.

2 Place the oil-board shape on the cake, then mask the surrounding area of cake with paper. Lightly spray the teddy bear with chestnut brown colour. Remove the paper and card.

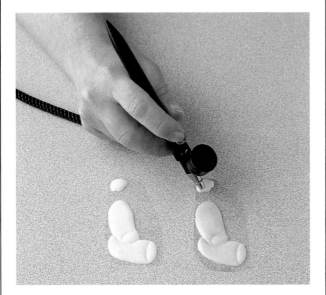

3 Run-out the arm, leg and nose with white icing. When completely dry spray with chestnut colour before removing the pieces from the wax paper. The force of the air brush can blow the small run-outs away if they are removed from the paper first.

4 Paint the details on the teddy bear and outline the edge with small lines to give a fur effect. Fix the run-out arm, leg and nose in position with icing.

TEDDY
OUTLINE

God
Bless
MARC

TOP DESIGN
AND TEMPLATE

RUN-OUT
TEMPLATES

LACE PIECES

SUSAN

PROFESSIONAL TIPS

Colour can be added to the petals by dampening the brush with diluted food colour instead of water.

◆

The choice of brush will depend on the size of the flowers or leaves.

◆

The icing should be soft peak consistency for brush embroidery. If it is too stiff the icing will dry quickly, too soft and it will flood rather than hold its shape.

INGREDIENTS

◆

25 × 20 cm (10 × 8 inch) oval Rich Fruit Cake, see page 138
apricot jam, boiled and sieved
1.25 kg (2½ lb) marzipan
1.5 kg (3 lb) Royal Icing, see page 139
selection of food colours
yellow petal dust
piping jelly
90 pieces Lace, see page 46

EQUIPMENT

◆

33 × 28 cm (13 × 11 inch) oval cake board
greaseproof (parchment) paper
scriber
thin cardboard
no. 2, 1, 0 and 00 piping tubes (tips)
paint brushes
1.25 metres (1½ yards) lace to trim board

ORDER OF WORK

◆

Cover the cake with marzipan, then coat it and the board with royal icing. Trace the design and inscription on a piece of greaseproof paper, then scribe it on the cake.

Cut an oval template from thin card. Place the template on the cake, pipe a small scroll design around the edge using a no. 0 tube.

Paint the leaves and flower stalks on the cake with food colour before beginning to work on the brush embroidered flowers.

Use a no. 1 tube to outline the petals and leaves, then brush the icing with a damp paint brush and leave to dry. Highlight the centre of the flowers with yellow petal dust. Pipe the inscription using a no. 1 tube and pink royal icing. Paint the detail around the capital letter with green colour to represent flower foliage.

Make a greaseproof paper pattern for the side of the cake, then scribe the extension work and flower design on the icing. Paint the leaves and rose hip with a fine brush. Complete the motif by adding the brush embroidered rose.

Pipe the bridge and tiered extension work (using no. 2, 1 and 00 tubes) with fresh pink royal icing, making each layer paler in colour. Complete the top edge of the extension work with a loop of white royal icing piped using a no. 0 tube. Lastly, attach the heart-shaped lace to the edge of the cake. Trim the board with lace.

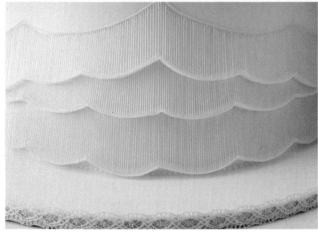

BRUSH EMBROIDERY

1 Scribe the design on the cake or plaque. Add 5 ml (1 teaspoon) of clear piping jelly to royal icing, the jelly will slow down the speed at which the icing sets, allowing more time for the icing to be brushed into place.

2 Painted leaves and some flower stems give depth. Begin the brush embroidery on areas that appear farthest away. Pipe a leaf outline using a no. 1 tube. Brush icing towards the centre vein. Draw the damp brush down the leaf to form the vein.

3 Do not outline more than one petal at a time. The tube size depends on the size of the flower: a no. 1 tube is used here. Outline the petal with icing, then brush it towards the flower's centre.

4 Pipe and brush each petal in turn. When the icing has dried, the flowers and leaves can be highlighted with powdered colour or they can be painted before the stamens are piped.

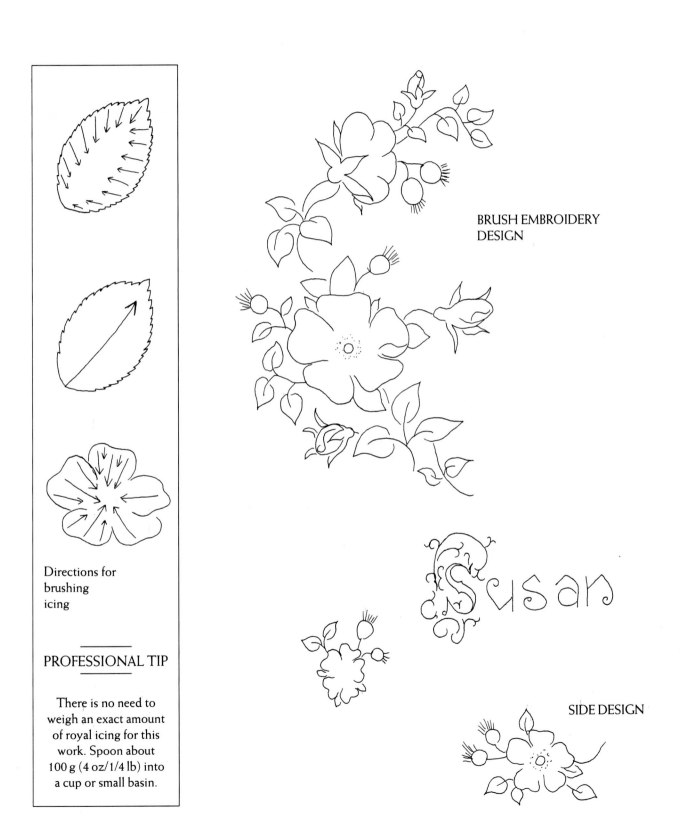

Directions for
brushing
icing

PROFESSIONAL TIP

There is no need to
weigh an exact amount
of royal icing for this
work. Spoon about
100 g (4 oz/1/4 lb) into
a cup or small basin.

BRUSH EMBROIDERY
DESIGN

Susan

SIDE DESIGN

BEST WISHES

MAIN SKILLS

Line Picture
Oriental String Work

◆

ADDITIONAL SKILLS

Marzipan Coating,
see page 10
Royal Icing Coating,
see page 56
Diagonal Extension Work with Bridge,
see page 33
Cut-out Blossom,
see page 119

◆

Design and Templates, see page 83

PROFESSIONAL TIPS

Use a no. 1 tube for the dominant lines in the picture and a no. 0 tube for smaller details.

◆

Use a damp paint brush to neaten the beginning and end of each piped line.

◆

Adding liquid glucose will make the icing more 'elastic' which is an advantage when piping oriental string work.

INGREDIENTS

◆

20 × 15 cm (8 × 6 inch) Rich Fruit Cake, see page 138
apricot jam, boiled and sieved
875 g (1¾ lb) marzipan
1.25 kg (2½ lb) Royal Icing, see page 139
selection of food colours
liquid glucose (clear corn syrup)
12 Cut-out Blossom (small and medium), see page 119

EQUIPMENT

◆

28 × 23 cm (11 × 9 inch) oval cake board
H pencil
greaseproof (parchment) paper
scriber
no. 2, 1, 0 and 00 piping tubes (tips)
set square
0.75 metre (1 yard) ribbon to trim board

ORDER OF WORK

◆

Cover the cake with marzipan. Coat the cake and board with white royal icing.

Trace the line picture and inscription, then scribe them on the cake. Make a greaseproof paper pattern for the side of the cake, then scribe the bridge work, embroidery and divisions for the oriental string work on the cake.

Build out the bridge work using no. 2, 1 and 0 tubes and pink royal icing. The extension strands are piped with a no. 00 tube.

Pipe the oriental string work in pink and white royal icing using a no. 0 tube. Pipe the embroidery on the top and side of the cake with the same icing.

Pipe the picture and inscription in the appropriate colours. In this case, this skill was left until last because the cake is turned upside down to pipe the oriental string work. Care must be taken not to knock the border when piping the picture.

Lastly, attach the blossom to the board with a little icing and pipe the leaves. Trim the board with ribbon.

LINE PICTURE

◆

Two examples have been described to show how this technique can be developed. Make the icing colours bright so that they contrast well with each other. The outlines are not as clear if pale colours are used. Oriental string work is quick, therefore a useful way to decorate a cake.

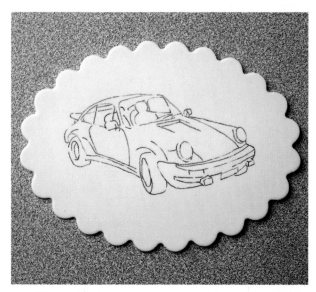

1 Trace the design on greaseproof paper, using an H pencil. Carefully re-draw the details on the reverse side of the paper. Scribe the design through the pattern on the dry cake or plaque.

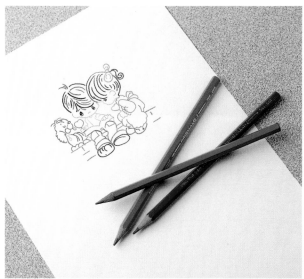

4 This design incorporates many colours. The colours in the illustration indicate the colour of icing to use.

OUTLINE FOR CAR DESIGN

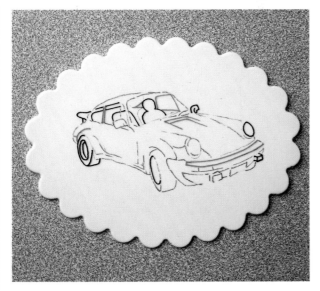

2 Using a no. 0 tube, begin by piping the details that appear furthest away in the design. Make sure the scribed line is covered by the icing, using a damp brush to ease the icing in place. Pipe any small details with this tube.

3 Use a no. 1 tube to pipe the more prominent lines. The change in tube size will help to create dimension within the picture.

5 Trace the design on the cake or plaque. Using a no. 1 or 0 tube, begin piping the lines which appear furthest away, refer to the template illustration for colour sequence.

6 Use a damp brush to neaten the lines where they join. Continue to pipe over the scribed lines until the picture is complete.

ORIENTAL STRING WORK

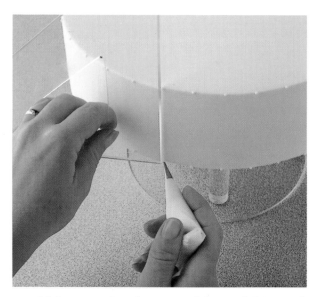

1 Make a template the size and shape of the top of the cake. Divide the circumference in equal portions about 1 cm (½ inch) apart. Place the template on the cake and mark the divisions with dots. Use a set square to line up the lower set of piped dots.

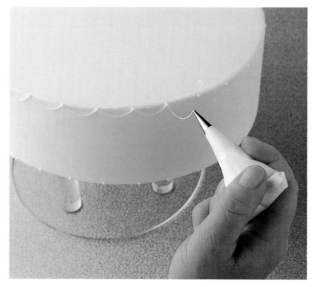

2 Stir 5 ml (1 teaspoon) liquid glucose into a cup of fresh royal icing. Use a no. 1 tube to pipe loops from dot to dot. The loops should not touch the side of the cake but they should hang freely from the dots. Allow to dry.

3 Turn the cake upside down, supporting it on a perfectly clean stand which is smaller than the cake. Pipe a row of loops between the dots around the cake base. Pipe a second row of loops around the cake top. Allow to dry.

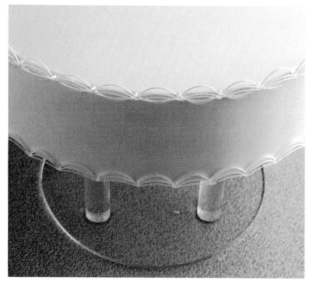

4 Turn the cake the right way up. Repeat the process of piping loops several times, making each row of loops slightly shorter than the previous row.

TOP DESIGN AND TEMPLATE

EMBROIDERY

HAPPY DAYS

MAIN SKILL

Run-out Collar

◆

ADDITIONAL SKILLS

Marzipan Coating,
see page 10
Royal Icing Coating,
see page 56
Run-out Figures,
see page 50
Painting on Sugar,
see page 26
Using an Air Brush,
see page 72
Graduated Line Piping, see page 92

◆

Design and Templates, see pages
86/88/89

INGREDIENTS

◆

20 × 15 cm (8 × 6 inch) oval Rich Fruit Cake, see page 138
apricot jam, boiled and sieved
875 g (1¾ lb) marzipan
1.5 kg (3 lb) Royal Icing, see page 139
small amount of Flower Paste, see page 140
petal dust colours
selection of food colours
egg white to thin icing (optional)

EQUIPMENT

◆

25 × 20 cm (12 × 10 inch) oval cake board
wax paper
greaseproof (parchment) paper
spray adhesive
masking tape
no. 1 and 0 piping tubes (tips)
scalpel
1 metre (1 yard) ribbon to trim board
glass or firm board to dry run-outs
lamp (angle-poise)
cranked pallet knife
scriber
air brush

ORDER OF WORK

◆

Cover the cake with marzipan. Coat the cake and board with royal icing.

Run-out the top and bottom collars on wax paper and leave to dry under a lamp. Remove the collar from the wax paper and pipe a picot edge around it using a no. 0 tube. Cut-out the daisy, leaf, and butterfly from rolled-out flower paste and leave to dry, then brush with petal dust.

Use the appropriate colours to run-out the mice on wax paper, then lay the figures for the side of the cake to dry over the side of the oval cake tin in which the cake was baked, this will make the run-outs dry slightly curved making them easier to fix in place. When the run-out mice are dry remove them from the wax paper and paint on the details.

Use a paper pattern to scribe the background design on the top and side of the cake. Use an air brush to lightly spray a hint of green to represent grass. Paint the remaining details with food colour.

Carefully secure the collar and cake to the iced board. Pipe a small dot border around the base of the cake using a no. 1 tube.

Secure the run-out figures to the cake with royal icing. Use green icing to pipe the tufts of grass on wax paper, when dry attach them to the board with a dot of icing. Finally, position the top collar on the cake and pipe two rows of graduated line work to outline the collar design. Trim the board with ribbon.

RUN-OUT COLLARS

SIDE DESIGN

PROFESSIONAL TIPS

Use a no. 1 tube to flood the icing on the collar as the small aperture breaks any air bubbles in the icing.

♦

The gentle heat of the lamp dries the icing quickly creating a shiny surface. However, too much heat may dissolve the wax on the paper and prevent the run-out releasing when dry.

♦

Cut the centre of the wax paper to release the tension caused by the icing contracting slightly when drying. If the paper is not cut, the collar may crack and break.

1 Stick the pattern of the collar to the glass or board, preferably using spray adhesive. Place a sheet of wax paper over the pattern and tape the edge down. Make sure there are no creases or ripples in the paper as they will make the collar uneven.

4 Cut a cross in the wax paper with a scalpel to release the tension in the paper, taking care not to disturb the collar. Place under a lamp to dry.

2 Thin some royal icing with egg white or water. Draw a knife through the icing to check the consistency: the icing should return to its own level by the count of eight.

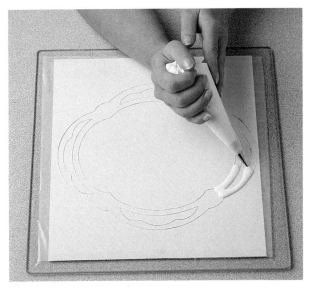

3 Prepare 2 large piping bags fitted with no. 1 tubes and half fill them with the prepared run-out icing. Begin flooding the outline of the collar; work 5 cm (2 inches) clockwise, then 5 cm (2 inches) anti-clockwise and so on. This avoids joins.

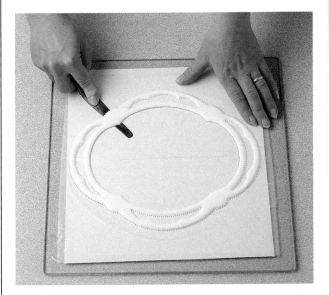

5 Remove the dry collar from the wax paper by gently sliding a thin cranked palette knife under it. When the collar has been released, leave it on the paper and pipe the picot edge using a no. 0 tube. Release the collar as before.

6 Use a no. 1 tube to pipe a line of soft peak icing around the edge of the cake. Lift the collar on the cake, then outline the inside edge of the cake with graduated line piping, this is to disguise any minor flaws in shape between the collar and the cake.

TOP DESIGN

SIDE DESIGN

COLLAR TEMPLATE

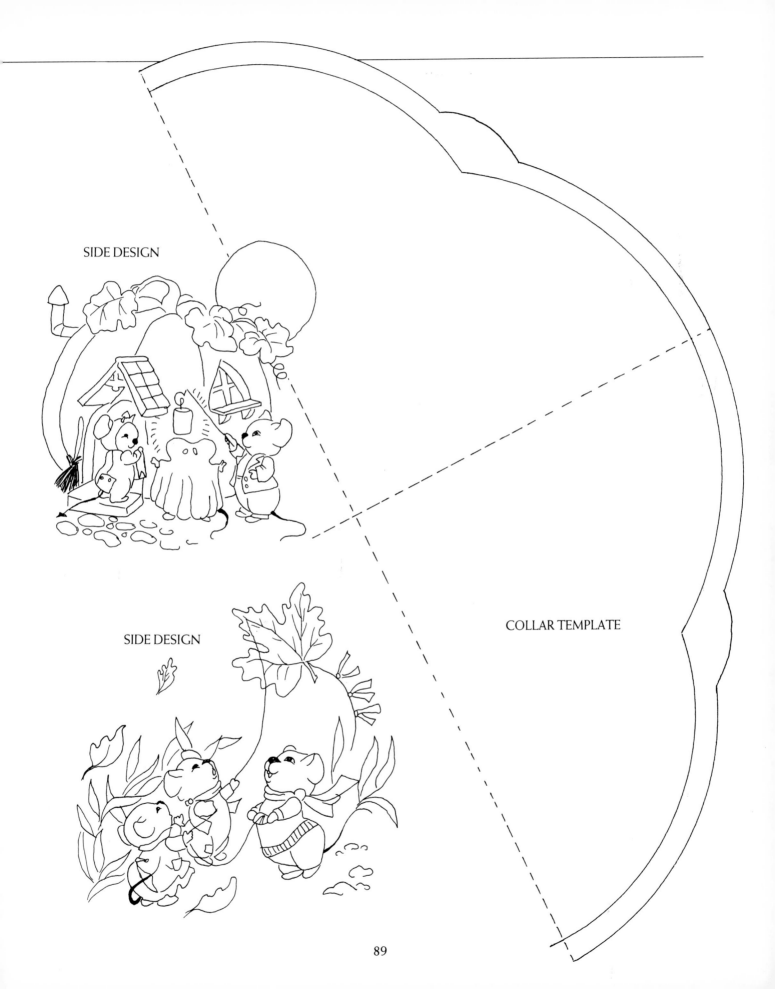

SIDE DESIGN

SIDE DESIGN

COLLAR TEMPLATE

89

FOR YOU MUM

INGREDIENTS

♦

20 × 15 cm (8 × 6 inch) oval Rich Fruit
Cake, see page 138 (or
use a dummy)
apricot jam, boiled and sieved (not
required for a dummy)
875 g (1¾ lb) marzipan (not required
for a dummy)
1.5 kg (3 lb) Royal Icing, see page 139
2 Edible Ribbon Bows, see page 40
about 30 Cut-out Blossom (small),
see page 119
about 10 miniature Roses, see
page 128
selection of food colours

EQUIPMENT

♦

33 × 28 cm (13 × 11 inch) oval cake
board
wax paper
lamp (angle-poise)
cranked palette knife
no. 2, 1 and 0 piping tubes (tips)
greaseproof (parchment) paper
scriber
H pencil
1.25 metres (1½ yards) ribbon to
trim board

ORDER OF WORK

♦

Cover the cake with marzipan. Coat the dummy or cake and board with
royal icing. Coat the board with royal icing.

Run-out the two top collars, dog and girl's figure on wax paper. Leave to
dry under a lamp, then use a cranked palette knife to remove them from
the wax paper. Use a no. 1 tube to pipe dots to secure the top
collar pieces together.

Cut a paper pattern for the side of the cake, then scribe the embroidery
design on the cake and leave the pattern in place. Place the cake in the
stand to pipe the graduated line work, then remove the pattern and pipe
the embroidery.

Place a template of the outside collar edge on the cake board, making sure
it is in the correct position, in line with the side design on the cake.
Outline the template with graduated line piping.

Secure the cake to the board and neaten the bottom edge with a piped
shell border using a no. 2 tube. Scribe the inscription on the cake and pipe
it using a no. 1 tube and pink royal icing. Paint the dog and figure with
food colour, then place them and the flowers on the cake. Add the ribbons
to the figure. When they are arranged correctly, secure them with icing.

Finally, position the two collars on the cake. Outline the inside collar edge
with graduated line piping. Trim the board with ribbon.

SIDE PIPING
(Graduated Line Piping)

◆

This stand is only required when the design or line piping defies gravity. This piece of equipment is used mainly for exhibition work, for unusual designs, when dummies are used and the weight of the cake is not a problem. For example, when piping loops, gravity makes the icing drop into shape. On this design the side-facing loops are difficult to pipe accurately. Also, piping the top loops involves turning the cake upside down several times without the stand. Many line designs which do not require the stand can be used on the side of a cake but always remember to allow for gravity when planning your design.

PROFESSIONAL TIPS

When piping graduated line work the aim is to pipe each row of icing as close to the previous row as possible without having the lines touching.

◆

Use contiguous tube sizes for graduated line work, for example 3, 2, 1 or 2, 1, 0.

1 The adjustable stand holds any depth of cake. Care must be taken when a real cake is being decorated: the sponges will help to grip and support the cake but large, heavy cakes are difficult to support.

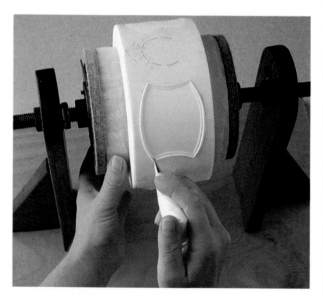

4 Overpipe the first piped line with a no. 1 tube, then pipe another line on the inside edge of each pattern. The stand makes this design easier to execute.

2 Cut a greaseproof pattern the depth of the cake, then fold it into four equal pieces and draw the design accurately on each section. Cut out the portion for the line piping and trace the embroidery on both sides of the paper using an H pencil.

3 Secure the pattern firmly around the side of the cake, making sure it is in the correct position. Place the coated cake (or dummy) in the stand. Trace the embroidery on the cake using a scriber. Outline each cut away shape with a no. 2 tube.

5 Use a no. 0 tube and pink royal icing to overpipe the two previous lines of icing. Pipe a third row on the inside edge of each pattern. A damp brush can be used to help to neaten icing joins.

6 Remove the paper template, then use a no. 0 tube to pipe the embroidery with pale green and pink royal icing. Reduce some pink royal icing to run-out consistency and pipe the bows directly on the cake. The run-out icing must not be too thin as this may result in small holes forming on the surface of the bows. Since they are run-out directly on the cake surface any flaws will be difficult to rectify or disguise.

Remember that the piped flower embroidery should be piped using full peak icing, with a no. 0 tube.

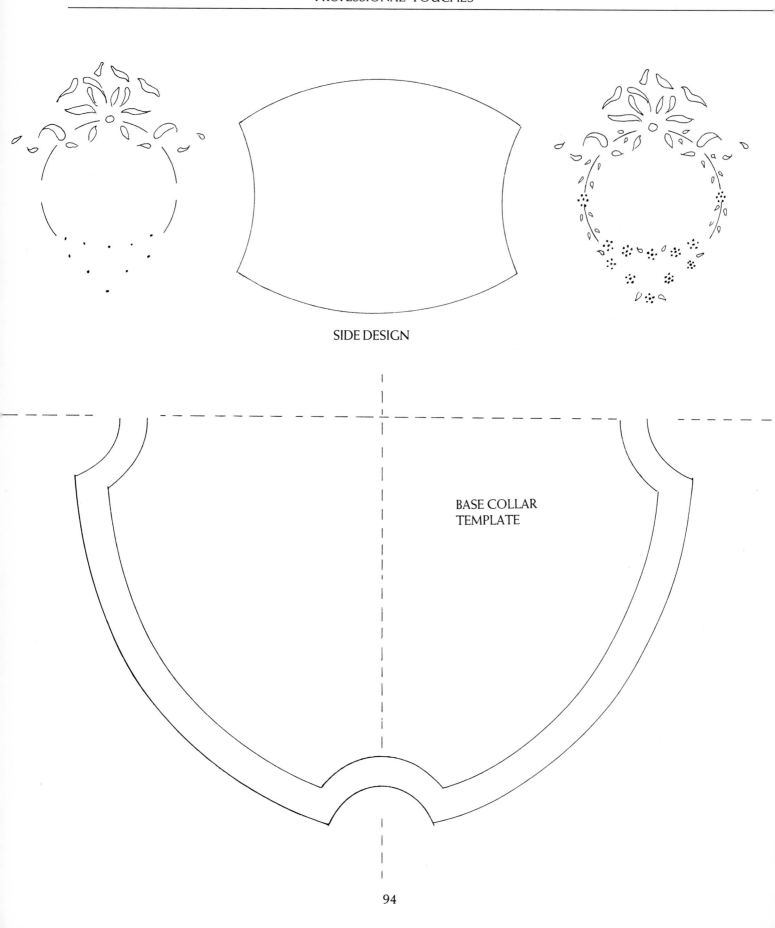

SIDE DESIGN

BASE COLLAR
TEMPLATE

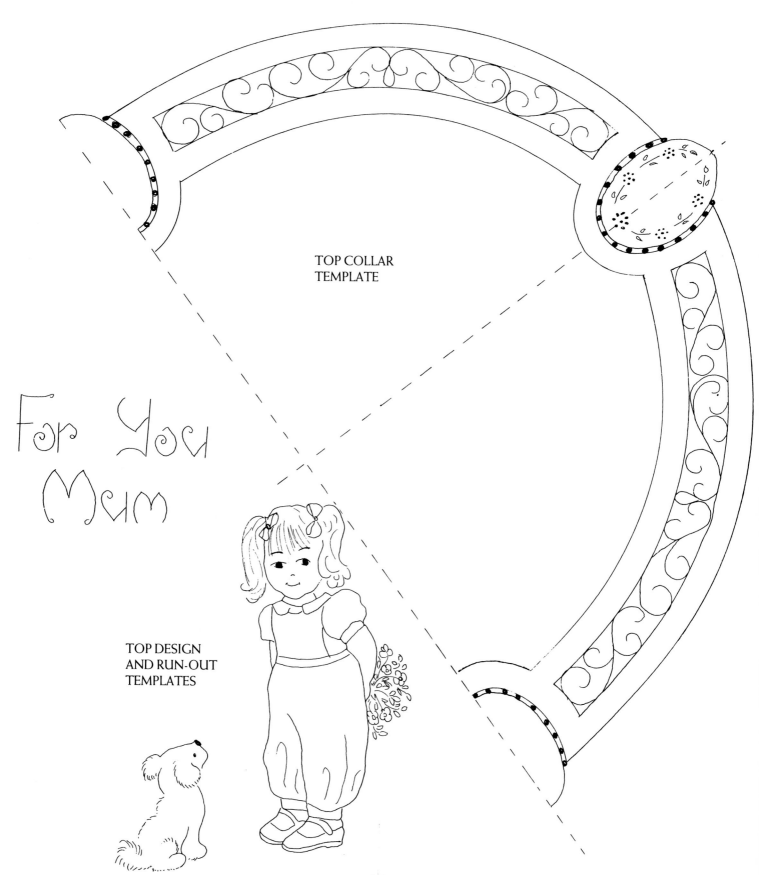

TOP COLLAR
TEMPLATE

For You
Mum

TOP DESIGN
AND RUN-OUT
TEMPLATES

SPRING MEDLEY

INGREDIENTS

◆

25 × 20 cm (10 × 8 inch) oval and 13 cm (5 inch) round Rich Fruit Cakes, see page 138
apricot jam, boiled and sieved
1.75 kg (3½ lb) marzipan
clear alcohol (gin or vodka)
2.25 kg (4½ lb) sugarpaste
icing (confectioner's) sugar for rolling out
750 g (1½ lb) Royal Icing, see page 139
Lace pieces: bottom tier 110, top tier 60, pillars 54, see page 46
small amount of Flower Paste, see page 140
egg white for dampening paste
6 Open Roses, see page 126
12 Roses, see page 128
18 Daphne sprays, see pages 119/136
18 Cut-out Daphne, see page 119
white vegetable fat for rolling out
12 wired Double Blossom, see note on page 118

EQUIPMENT

◆

33 × 28 cm (13 × 11 inch) oval cake board
18 cm (7 inch) round cake board
scriber
no. 1, 0 and 00 piping tubes (tips)
rolling pin • smoothers
3 hollow 9 cm (3½ inch) perspex tubes
greaseproof (parchment) paper
cellophane paper
4 wooden dowels
bunch of dried gypsophila
3 metres (3¼ yards) ribbon to trim boards

ORDER OF WORK

◆

Cover the cakes with marzipan and pale pink sugarpaste. Cover the boards with sugarpaste. Secure the cakes to the boards when dry.

Scribe the embroidery and extension work design around the sides of the cakes. Use a no. 0 tube and white royal icing to pipe the embroidery. Using a no. 1 tube, pipe a small shell border around the base of each cake. Use the same bag of icing to pipe the bridge loops. When the loops are dry attach them to the cake, then pipe the extension strands using a no. 00 tube and fresh white royal icing. Attach the lace pieces.

Prepare the cake pillars and top decoration. Carefully skewer the bottom tier with the pieces of dowel and cut each wooden dowel (in turn) to length: they must be slightly longer than the combined measurement of cake and pillars. The weight of the top tier must be on the dowelling *not* on the pillars to prevent the pillars breaking.

Assemble the flower sprays on the cakes to establish the correct size and shape. Insert the flower wires and stems in a piece of sugarpaste. Wires must never be allowed to penetrate the cake coating. Attach the single blossoms to the cake and boards. Trim the boards with ribbon.

PASTILLAGE CAKE PILLARS

◆

These pillars can be made to match the colour of the cake perfectly. The weight of each tier must be supported on wooden dowel.

EMBROIDERY

PROFESSIONAL TIPS

Use fresh egg white for the run-out icing as this will give the back of the run-out a shiny surface.

◆

Cellophane paper can be used for run-out work, as it is transparent the design can be seen easily. Ensure that it is non-permeable or the run-out may stick to it.

◆

Make several extra pillars and select the best match for the cake.

1 Roll out the flower paste on a lightly greased board. Trim the paste to the same length as the perspex tube, then dampen it with egg white. Roll the paste around the tube.

4 Trace the shape of the pillar ends and cover securely with cellophane. Outline the circle using a no. 1 tube, then flood the outside edge (not the centre). Stand the pillar in the soft icing. When dry, repeat for the other end.

2 Cut off the excess paste, ensuring that the ends fit together without overlapping. Use a smoother to gently roll the pillar until the paste is smooth. Trim both ends level before leaving to dry.

3 Cut a piece of greaseproof paper the width and length of the pillar. The design illustrated makes a spiral pattern. Scribe the design accurately on each pillar.

5 Use a no. 00 tube to pipe the lace pieces, then attach them to the pillar with dots of icing when dry.

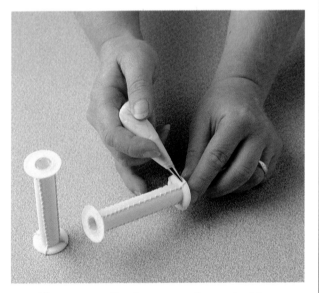

6 Alternative pillar designs can be made. Use a no. 1 tube and orange icing to pipe four lines on each pillar, then use a no. 0 tube and white icing to pipe a zig-zag design over the orange line. This design is not as fragile as the lace pieces.

'C' TOP DECORATION

1 Draw a 'C' shape, about 10 cm (4 inches) high. Roll out a length of flower paste using a smoother to obtain an even shape. Position the paste over the design, then leave to dry. Cut out a small disc of paste on which to assemble the decoration.

2 Pipe a rope of royal icing on the disc of paste and attach the 'C' shape. Support the 'C' with a folded piece of paper which has a small slit cut in the fold until the icing has dried.

3 Place a small ball of sugarpaste over the base of the 'C'. Place the cake on a turntable. Assemble the decoration on the cake: begin by inserting the sprays of dried gypsophila, then gently insert the wires of the roses into the soft sugarpaste.

4 Continue to add the flowers to build up the required shape. Tweezers are useful for handling the smaller flowers. Keep turning the cake around to create an even arrangement.

FOR YOUR BABY

INGREDIENTS

◆

25 × 20 cm (10 × 8 inch) oval Rich
Fruit Cake, see page 138
apricot jam, boiled and sieved
1.25 kg (2½ lb) marzipan
clear alcohol (gin or vodka)
1.75 kg (3½ lb) sugarpaste
750 g (1½ lb) Royal Icing made with
fresh egg white, see page 139
selection of food colours
14 Apple Blossom, see page 129
120 pieces Lace, see page 46
Mexican Paste, see page 140, mixed
with an equal quantity sugarpaste
white vegetable fat for rolling out
confectioner's varnish

EQUIPMENT

◆

33 × 28 cm (13 × 11 inch) oval cake
board
1 metre (1 yard) narrow pale pink
ribbon
no. 1, 0 and 00 piping tubes (tips)
greaseproof (parchment) paper
scriber • fine paint brushes
wax paper
spray adhesive
masking tape
rolling pin
small piece of sponge (foam)
glass or firm board to dry run-outs
1.25 metres (1½ yards) lace to trim
board edge

ORDER OF WORK

◆

Cover the cake with marzipan. Cover the cake and board with white sugarpaste. When the coating has dried, secure the cake to the board with a small amount of icing. Fill any gaps between the cake and board with icing before securing the narrow ribbon to the base of the cake. Use a no. 0 tube to pipe a picot edge on the board. Make a greaseproof pattern for the side of the cake. Fold the paper into 6 equal portions, then trace the design on each section. Keep all pencil lines on one side.

Place the pattern around the cake with the pencil marks outside and scribe the design on the cake. Paint the stems and some of the small leaves on the side of the cake. Brush-embroider the larger leaves. Run-out the blue birds with white icing on wax paper. When dry paint the birds with food colour and secure them and the flowers to the cake with dots of icing.

Pipe the bridgeless extension work using a no. 00 tube and white icing. Coat the cake 4 days ahead of beginning extension work so that the sugarpaste is firm enough not to mark easily if touched but still soft enough for the pins to be inserted easily. Attach the lace pieces to the cake with white royal icing. Scribe the inscription on the cake and use a no. 0 tube and pink royal icing to pipe over the scribed lines.

Prepare the cradle; it is not necessary to secure it and it is also easier to transport, if necessary, separately. Trim the board.

MAKING THE CRADLE

1 Secure the design to the glass or board with spray adhesive. Tape wax paper tightly over the design. Run-out the three pieces of the cradle and leave to dry under a lamp. Remove the run-out pieces from the paper with a cranked pallet knife.

PROFESSIONAL TIPS

Mixing Mexican paste and sugarpaste together produces a pliable paste which sets hard.

◆

Make cardboard templates from the design as they are easier to cut around and they will not mark the paste as easily as paper.

◆

Confectioner's varnish seals the back of the run-out. Icing made with egg white substitute (albumen) will absorb the varnish and it may stain the icing.

4 Roll out the mixed paste as thinly as possible on a lightly greased board. Use the template to cut out the drapes. Cut the embroidery design with a no. 0 tube. While the paste is still pliable, pleat the top edge.

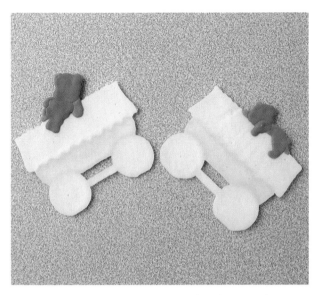

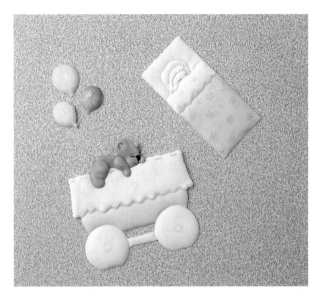

2 Use fresh egg white to make the royal icing. Paint the back of the teddy bear with confectioner's varnish. When the varnish is dry, run-out the back of the bears to make double-sided run-outs.

3 Paint the details on the run-outs with a fine brush and selection of food colours, taking care to keep the brush nearly dry to prevent the run-outs for losing their gloss.

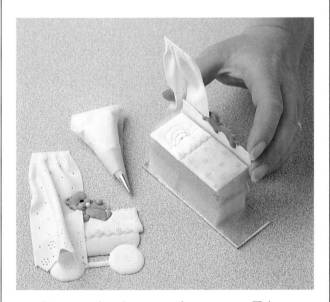

5 Position the drape on the run-out. Take care that the tops of the drapes line up together, then secure to the run-out with royal icing and allow to dry. Make 3 bows from the excess paste. The candle is ready for assembling.

6 Assemble the cradle by placing the run-out centre piece on a block of sponge cut to the correct height. Use a no. 1 tube to pipe icing along each side of the cradle and the drape top. Dry the assembled cradle before adding balloons and details.

TEMPLATES FOR CRADLE

REVERSE RUN-OUTS

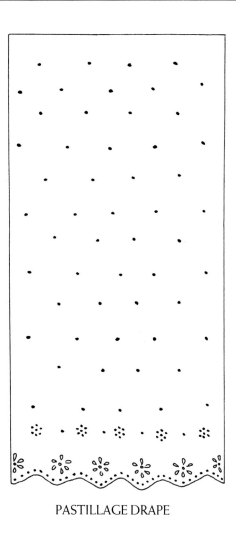

PASTILLAGE DRAPE

RUN-OUT TEMPLATES

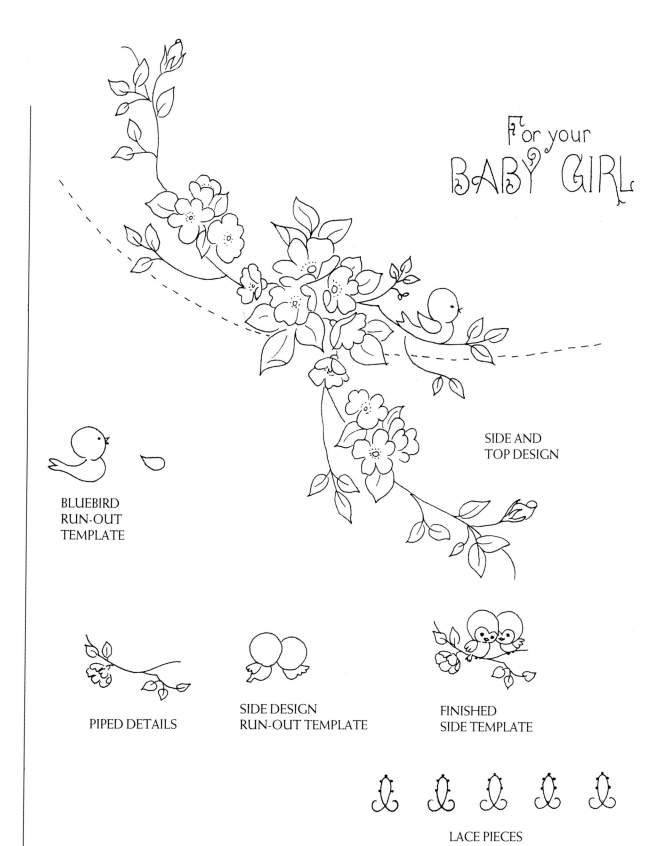

For your
BABY GIRL

SIDE AND
TOP DESIGN

BLUEBIRD
RUN-OUT
TEMPLATE

PIPED DETAILS

SIDE DESIGN
RUN-OUT TEMPLATE

FINISHED
SIDE TEMPLATE

LACE PIECES

THE BRIDE CAKE

INGREDIENTS

♦

23 × 13 cm (9 × 6 inch) elongated hexagonal Rich Fruit Cake, see page 138
apricot jam, boiled and sieved
1 kg (2 lb) marzipan
clear alcohol (gin or vodka)
1.25 kg (2½ lb) sugarpaste
500 g (1 lb) Royal Icing, see page 139
selection of food colours
100 pieces Lace, see page 46
10 Roses, see page 128

14 Blossom Sprays, see pages 119/136
6 Daphne Sprays, see pages 119/136

EQUIPMENT

♦

28 × 23 cm (11 × 8 inch) oval board
scriber
paint brushes of various sizes
no. 1, 0 and 00 piping tubes (tips)
greaseproof (parchment) paper
sterile pins
small posy pick (suitable for food use)
1 metre (1 yard) ribbon to trim board

ORDER OF WORK

♦

Cover the cake with marzipan and sugarpaste. Leave for about 4 days to dry. Cover the board with sugarpaste. Secure the cake to the board.

Scribe the picture of the bride and bridesmaid on the cake. Paint the faces, arms and legs with flesh coloured food colour, reduced with water, and paint the hair.

Begin the brush embroidery by outlining the part of the dress which appears furthest away, then brush the royal icing in the direction of the folds in the fabric. Gradually build out the dress, applying heavier pressure on the piping bag for parts of the dress that are more prominent. Complete the figure by painting a fine brown outline around the painted areas. Pipe embroidery for the headdresses and bridesmaid's bouquet.

Make a greaseproof paper pattern for the side of the cake and scribe the extension work design through the pattern. Using a no 1 tube, pipe a small shell border around the base of the cake. Pipe the bridgeless extension work with fresh white royal icing.

Use a no. 0 tube and pink royal icing to pipe three tiny 'O' shapes for the embroidery and green shells to represent leaves. These must be evenly spaced. Pipe the drop loops between each bunch of flower embroidery. Attach the lace pieces to the cake at this stage.

Insert a small plastic pick into the cake to hold the flower spray but do not allow the wire to penetrate the coating. Trim the board with ribbon.

BRIDGELESS EXTENSION WORK

1 Insert sterile pin tips evenly around the cake, 5 mm (¼ inch) from the board. Brush melted white fat on pins. Using a no. 0 tube and fresh icing pipe loops from pin to pin: they must be even in length and distance from the cake. Leave to dry.

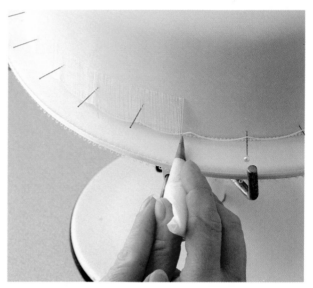

2 Use a no. 00 tube to pipe the threads of extension work. Do not damage the bridge loops. Remove the support pins as you progress. To pipe a second layer of extension work, replace the pins between the extension strands while the icing is pliable.

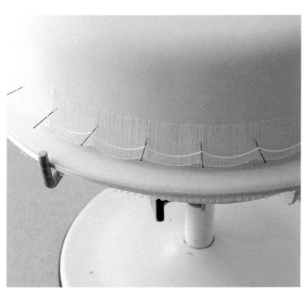

3 For the second layer of extension work pipe another row of loops from the greased pins. Take care to avoid touching the existing extension work with the second layer of loops.

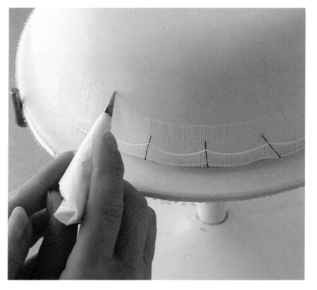

4 Tilt the cake towards you and pipe the second row of extension work, removing the pins as you work around the cake. This work is mainly used on exhibition cakes where the competitor is showing a difficult skill.

BRUSH EMBROIDERY DESIGN
AND TEMPLATE

EMBROIDERY

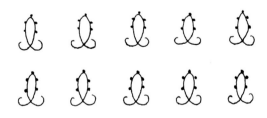

LACE PIECES

WEDDING BELLS

INGREDIENTS

◆

28 cm (11 inch), 20 cm (8 inch) and
13 cm (5 inch) Rich Fruit Cakes, see
page 138
apricot jam, boiled and sieved
4 kg (8 lb) marzipan
clear alcohol (gin or vodka)
5.25 kg (10½ lb) sugarpaste
Edible Ribbon pieces: bottom tier
100, middle tier 90, top tier 80, see
page 40
confectioner's varnish
Royal Icing for extension work, see
page 139
8 Pastillage Pillars, see page 98
Lace pieces: bottom tier 400, middle
tier 90, top tier 80, see page 46
12 Flower Sprays, see page 136
12 Edible Ribbon Bows, see page 40
12 each large, medium and
small Cut-out Blossom, see page 119

TOP DECORATION

500 g (1 lb) Flower Paste or Mexican
Paste, see page 140
egg white
17 Roses, see page 128
28 Lilac, see page 120
28 pulled filler flowers, see page 118
small amount of sugarpaste
white vegetable fat for rolling out

EQUIPMENT

◆

38 cm (15 inch), 28 cm (11 inch) and
20 cm (8 inch) square cake boards
8 wooden dowels plus extra for
drying ribbon loops
greaseproof (parchment) paper
no. 1, 0 and 00 piping tubes (tips)
rolling pin • thin cardboard • scalpel

ORDER OF WORK

◆

Cover the cakes with marzipan and coat the cake boards with sugarpaste.
Prepare the pieces of edible ribbon, varnish and dry each piece. Work on
one cake at a time: first coat it with white sugarpaste and place it on the
coated board. Make a paper pattern, deeper than the cake so that the
points fold over the top edge. Tape the pattern in place. Insert the ribbon
in the fresh paste, remove the pattern and leave to dry.

Scribe the bell design on the cake. Use a no. 0 tube to pipe a shell border
around the base of each cake. Use the same tube to pipe the bell design.
Mark the position of the pillars on the bottom and middle tiers. Cut 4
pieces of wooden dowel for each tier to the same length: they must be
slightly longer than the combined measurement of the cake depth and
pastillage pillars to prevent the pillars from cracking. Pipe the bridgeless
extension work using a no.0 or 00 tubes, and then attach the lace pieces.

Carefully secure the flower bouquets to the cake corners with a little royal
icing. Do not push the wire into the coating on the cakes. Neaten the top
of each bouquet with a sugar bowl. Place 3 cut-out blossom on each
embroidered bell design. Trim the boards with ribbon.

HEART TOP DECORATION

1 Roll out some flower paste or Mexican paste on a lightly greased board. Use a cardboard template and scalpel to cut out the heart-shaped pieces and base. Leave to dry flat. Place on wax paper. Use a no. 0 tube to pipe a picot border around each.

2 Assemble the heart pieces together and secure them with royal icing. It is easier to assemble the pieces upside-down. Leave to dry. Meanwhile tape the miniature sprays of sugar flowers together.

3 Use a little egg white to secure a ball of sugarpaste to the base of each heart piece. Carefully push the hearts into the soft sugarpaste. Use tweezers to position the flower sprays in the paste, adding extra flowers to make an attractive arrangement.

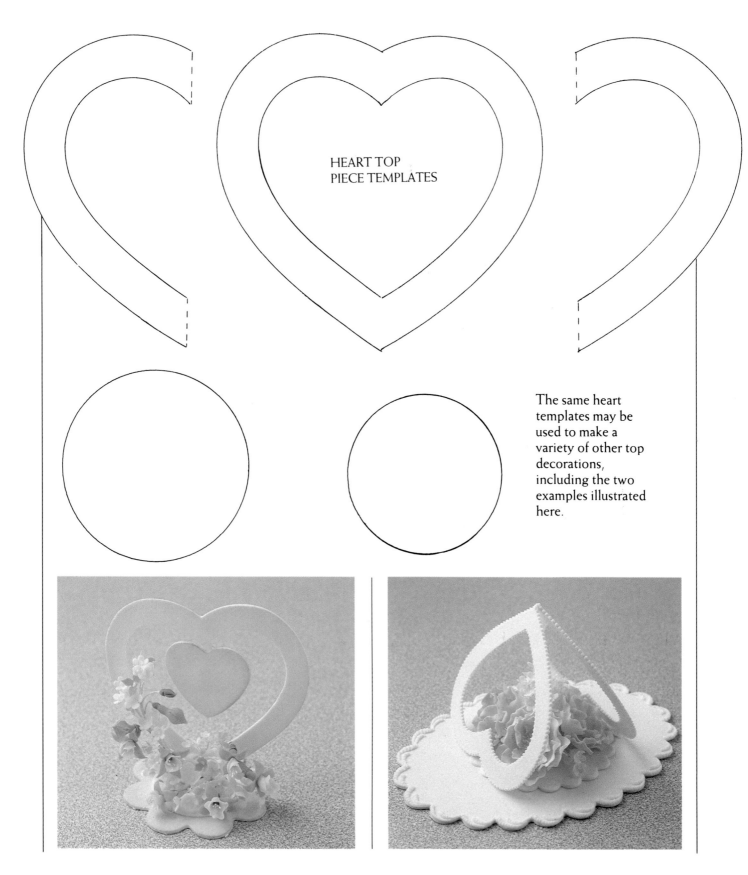

HEART TOP
PIECE TEMPLATES

The same heart
templates may be
used to make a
variety of other top
decorations,
including the two
examples illustrated
here.

MAKING BOUQUETS

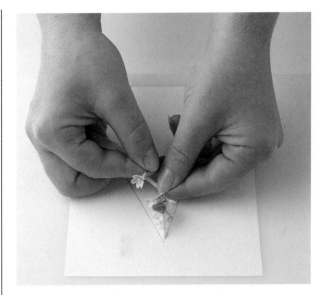

1 Draw the outline shape of each flower spray on a piece of paper, taking care that it is the right length for the cake. The bouquets are graduated in size according to the cakes.

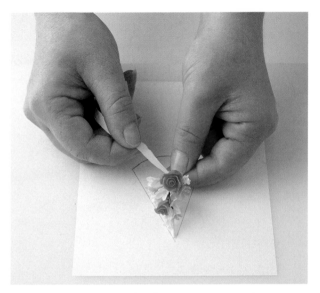

2 Begin by taping the flower wires together using a narrow strip of floristry tape. Keep matching the bouquet against the design as you work to obtain the correct shape and size.

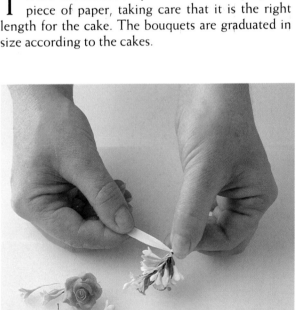

3 Stretch the floristry tape as you bind the flowers. The tape will stick when stretched. Handle the flowers carefully and remember that the back of the bouquet should look as neat as the front.

4 Finally, trim off excess wires as close as possible to the flowers. Never push wires into the coating on a cake. Always assemble flowers, or bouquets, in a posy pick or secure them to the cake with royal icing or on a piece of sugarpaste.

LACE PIECES

BELL DESIGN
TEMPLATES

SIDE TEMPLATE

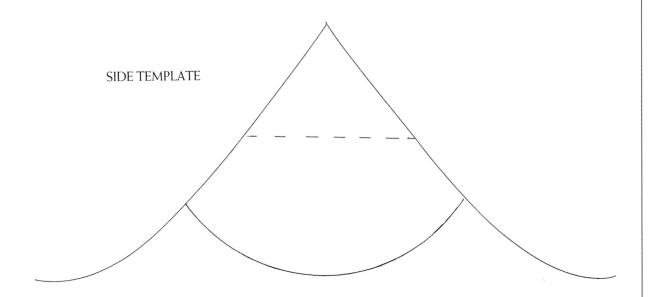

MAKING FLOWERS

EQUIPMENT

◆

non-stick board and rolling pin
selection of cutters
small sharp scissors
tweezers
28, 26 and 24 gauge wire
floristry tape
wooden dowel
cranked pallet knife
small piece of foam
stamens or cotton
scalpel
confectioner's varnish
white vegetable fat
petal dust
2 cm (¾ inch) brush
cocktail stick (toothpick)
cornflour (cornstarch) bag and icing
(confectioner's) sugar bag, see below
ball tool
bone tool
veining tool

PROFESSIONAL TIPS

A specialist product, spray vegetable fat,
is available from cake decorating
suppliers. It may be used instead of
confectioner's varnish for adding a shine
to flower paste items.

◆

To make a cornflour (cornstarch) or
icing (confectioner's) sugar bag, spoon
the dry ingredient into a clean stocking
and knot the end just above. This may
be used for finely dusting a surface.

This section provides instructions for making flowers that are used throughout the book. Flower Paste, see page 140, is used for making all the blooms.

◆

The first group of blooms, illustrated opposite, are cut out from paste rather than being moulded or pulled and they are the easiest to make. The instructions describe the method of making cut-out flowers with stamens; however the stamens do not have to be used. Many of the cakes in this book are decorated with flowers which do not have stamens, instead they have a spot of royal icing added to their centres.

◆

Double blossoms may be made by cutting out and shaping a flat blossom, then placing it on top of a blossom cut out and shaped as for the back of the fuchsia flower (see page 124, step 2). These are known as pulled cutter flowers, since they combine the use of cutters with hand shaping. Pulled filler flowers are tiny flowers used to complete sprays, bouquets or other arrangements on a cake.

◆

As well as the flowers, this section includes leaves and step-by-step instructions for making a spray of blackberries or loganberries, complete with blossom and leaves.

CUT-OUT FLOWERS

Blossom, Daphne and Primrose

1 Lightly grease a non-stick board with white vegetable fat. Roll out a small piece of flower paste very thinly, as above. Cut out the flowers and place them on a piece of sponge. Keep the paste covered with polythene to prevent it drying.

2 Shape the flowers on the sponge: place a ball tool on the centre of each flower and apply gentle pressure. Use a needle tool or hat pin to make a small hole in the middle of each flower. Leave to dry.

3 Thread a stamen through each dried flower and secure it in place by piping a dot of royal icing in the centre of the flower. Alternatively, pipe royal icing on the back of the flower around the stamen.

4 Cut or shred some floristry tape into thin strips. Tape three or four flowers to a piece of 28 gauge wire, keeping the flowers close together. The flowers can be brushed with petal dust in any colour.

LILAC

Lilac blossom is made by the pulled method which does not require cutters but a piece of pointed dowel and small sharp scissors are used. The spray of lilac illustrated consists of several small bunches of flowers taped together.

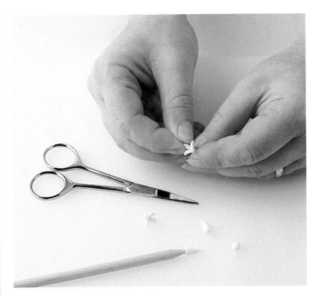

1 Roll a small ball of flower paste into a long thin tear-drop shape between your fingers. Dip the pointed end of a dowel in vegetable fat, then insert it in the rounded end of paste by about 1 cm (½ inch). Make 4 cuts for petals; pinch out petal tips.

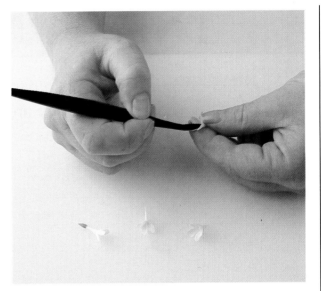

2 To shape the petals, put your thumb on the top of the petal and your index finger underneath, then gently slide your finger against your thumb to form the paste into the required shape. Thin each petal with a veining tool.

3 To make lilac buds, mould a small ball of paste into a tear-drop shape. Thread a stamen through the paste and gently roll the tip of the paste between your fingers. Mark 4 lines in the bud by cutting a cross with scissors.

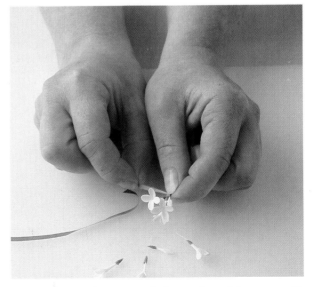

4 Make a calyx on each flower by adding a small piece of dark green paste. Tape the flowers and buds together with floristry tape. These flowers are very useful as fillers in arrangements of larger blooms.

NAZOMI ROSES

Nazomi roses are a particularly delicate variety of
wild rose and they are slightly smaller than the
ordinary wild rose.

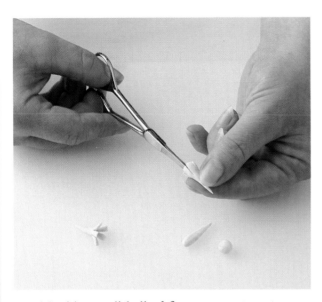

1   Mould a small ball of flower paste into a tear-drop shape. Push a greased dowel into the rounded end of the paste by about 5 mm (¼ inch). Remove the paste from the dowel and cut 5 petals. Open out the petals with your fingertips.

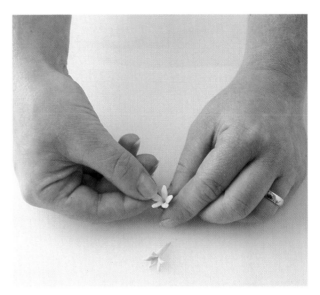

2   Place your thumb on top of the petal and your index finger underneath. Keep your thumb still, then stroke your finger against your thumb to stretch the paste and make the petal more delicate. Repeat for each petal.

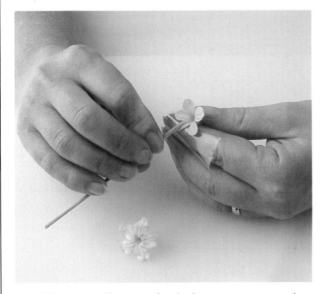

3   Wrap a small piece of polythene over your index finger. Rest the petal over your finger, then gently push a cocktail stick several times over each petal. This will add texture and frill the flower slightly.

4   Prepare the cotton stamens, page 127. Use 28 gauge wire. Thread the wire through the flower, neaten the flower back by rolling the paste between your index fingers, then remove excess. Cut a calyx from green paste and secure it with egg white.

FUCHSIA

1 Tape five stamens to 28 gauge wire, making one longer than the others. Cut 4 petals, frill their edges with a ball tool and cup their centres. Brush egg white on the right-hand side of each petal, then overlap them. Curl the petals around the stamens.

2 Shape a piece of contrasting paste into a 'light-bulb' shape. Roll out using a knitting needle. Use a calyx cutter to cut the fuchsia. Stroke the petal backs with a ball tool; hollow the centre with dowel. Brush egg white on the centre; slide on to wire.

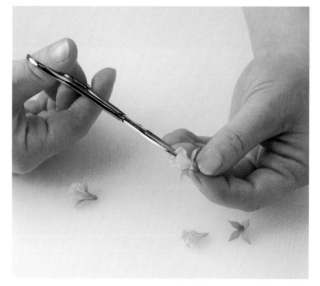

3 To make fuchsia buds, shape a tear-drop of paste. Thread a stamen through the paste. Holding the back of the bud, mark a cross in the paste with sharp scissors. When dry work a small ball of green paste on the back of the buds and flowers.

4 Do not wire the fuchsias to be arranged directly on a cake. Prepare the flower, then use a dowel to push the skirt petals into the calyx. Use sharp scissors to cut away a third of the flower away so that it will sit flat against the cake. Secure with icing.

LEAVES

Rose, Blackberry and Violet

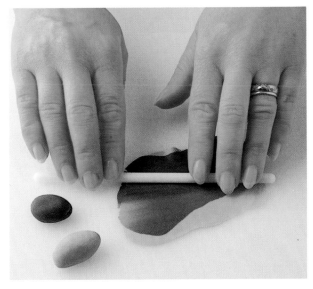

1 Roll out a piece of both light and dark green flower paste on a lightly greased board. Place the dark paste on top of the light green piece, roll each side of the paste as thinly as possible leaving a slightly thicker strip down the middle.

2 Rub white vegetable fat on the back of a fresh leaf. Place the leaf on the paste and apply gentle pressure, then use a scalpel to cut around the shape of the leaf. Remove the fresh leaf to leave the vein marks imprinted in the flower paste.

3 Hold the flower paste leaf between finger and thumb. Insert 26 gauge wire into the thicker part of the paste, then smooth the edge of the leaf with a bone tool. Twist the leaf slightly to give it movement and life, then allow to dry.

4 Use a 2 cm (¾ inch) brush and petal dust in a selection of colours to brush the colour from the edge towards the inside. Glaze leaves with confectioner's varnish. Alternatively, paint with oil or pass quickly through the steam of a boiling kettle.

OPEN ROSES

These roses have stamens made from cotton. Prepare the stamens as shown in step 1, dipping the ends of the cut cotton in white vegetable fat, then in fine cornmeal or semolina which has been coloured with petal dust.

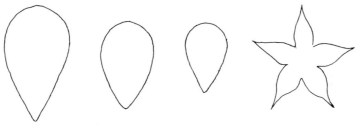

OPEN ROSE CUTTER TEMPLATES

1 Wind cream cotton loosely around a finger. Twist 28 gauge wire tightly through the loops. Remove the cotton and twist a second piece of wire through the other end. Cut the loops to make two bunches of stamens. Wind upright with wire.

2 Cover the stamen ends with paste. Colour 3 pieces of paste different shades. Using darkest shade and smallest cutter, cut 7 petals, cut 1 petal in strips. Rub the edge of each petal and cup the centres. Secure to stamens with egg white.

3 With flower upside down, paint pointed end of petals with egg white and secure to stem. Cut 6 more petals using medium and large cutters; middle and lightest paste. Frill and cup each petal. Add petals until the rose is the required size; dry.

4 Mould green paste into a 'light-bulb' shape. Roll out using a knitting needle. Cut out the calyx. Stroke the back of each point and hollow the centre with dowel. Brush egg white in the centre, then push on the rose wire.

ROSES

1   Roll a small piece of the darkest shade of paste in a ball. Thread hooked wire through the paste, then shape it into a cone. Use a cocktail stick to roll one side of the cone to make a flag shape. Brush with egg white, then wrap the flag tightly around cone.

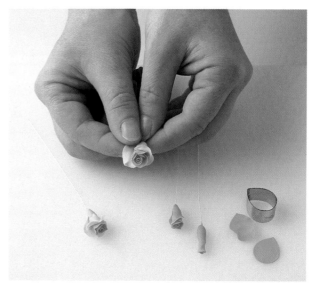

2   Cut 2 petals of dark paste, frill their edges and cup their centres. Brush egg white on the 'V' of petal, then attach to bud. Leave one side loose to tuck in second petal, then secure the edge. Add 2 petals in medium-coloured paste.

3   Make 3 petals of medium paste. Use a cocktail stick to curl back opposite corners on 2 petals and both corners of third. Brush 'V' with egg white. Overlap curled edges of 2 petals on rose. Cup third petal around back. More petals may be added.

4   Re-roll light and dark green paste thinly, lightest on top. Cut out calyx. Use a scalpel to make tiny cuts into edge; cup with ball tool. Brush centre with egg white and thread calyx on wire. Attach a small ball of paste to back of dry rose.

APPLE BLOSSOM

1 Mould some hoops of flower paste ready to shape the blossom and leave to dry. Roll out some green paste on a lightly greased board. Cut out the calyx, then gently cup its centre with a ball tool and place it over a hoop.

2 Roll out some white flower paste as thinly as possible (you should be able to read print through the paste). Cut out 5 petals and frill their edges, then cup their centres with a ball tool.

3 Brush egg white on the calyx. Overlap the petals as they are attached to the calyx. The first petal may need lifting slightly to insert the last petal to complete the spiral effect.

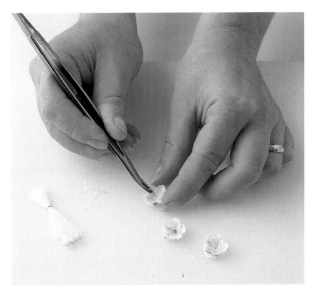

4 Using tweezers to insert as many tiny stamens around the centre as possible while the petals are still pliable. Complete the flower by adding a tiny ball of green paste. Accentuate the appearance of petals by brushing edges with pink petal dust.

VIOLETS

The combination of a large petal with the group of smaller ones is a key feature of violets. Notice that the end of the wire is hooked so that it buries itself firmly in the paste.

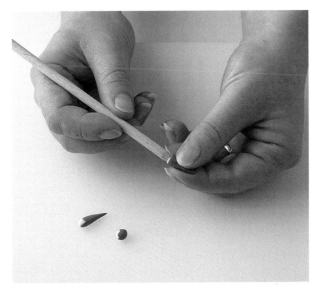

1 Roll a small piece of white and some violet-coloured paste into a ball. Shape into a long, thin tear-drop shape. Insert a greased dowel point into the rounded end, then cut one-third of the paste for the large petal. Cut the rest into 4 equal petals.

2 Shape the flower by pinching each corner of the petals together sideways. Place your thumb on the top of the petal and your finger underneath. Keep your thumb still, then stroke your finger against your thumb. Thin out petals gently with veining tool.

3 Make a small hook in 28 gauge wire and bend the hook over to make a golf club shape. Push the pointed end of the wire through the flower so the point comes out between the top 2 petals. Pull the wire back until the hook buries itself in the flower.

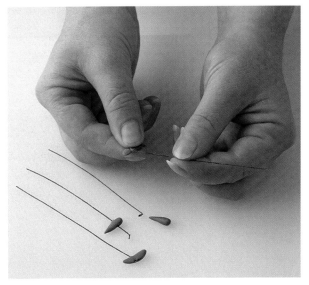

4 To make buds, mould a violet-coloured ball of paste into a tear-drop shape. Thread hooked wire through the side of the tear-drop until covered. Press a small strip of green paste over each bud back before bending the wire to represent the stalk.

LOGANBERRIES OR BLACKBERRIES

Use the template, see page 58, to prepare the leaves for this spray of blackberries, then wire the spray together with brown floristry tape. The same instructions may be used for making loganberries, although they tend to be slightly larger than blackberries and more red in colour.

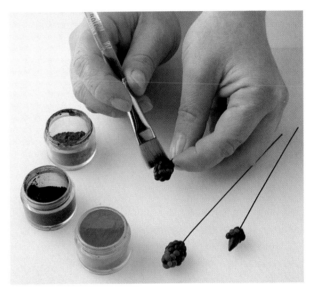

1 Place a pea-sized piece of paste on 26 gauge wire and shape it into a cone. Leave to dry. Colour several small pieces of paste, black, burgundy and green. Make the tiny berries from balls of paste. Thin some flower paste with egg white to make a glue.

2 Brush the 'glue' over the cone. Begin by attaching the berries at the wire end. When the cone is completely covered, leave to dry. Dab petal dust on the berry with a large soft brush.

3 Varnish the berry with confectioner's varnish. It may require two coats. When the varnish has dried, cut out a calyx from green flower paste and attach it to the berry with egg white.

4 Mould paste into 'light-bulb' shape. Roll out with knitting needle. Cut out calyx. Hollow out the centre with a dowel point. Cut 5 petals and frill edges with cocktail stick. Brush calyx with egg white. Attach petals and thread stamens.

MAKING THE BIBLE WITH SPRAY

◆

The distinct texture on the paste is achieved by rolling tapestry fabric over it. When the bible and spray of flowers are combined they make an attractive decoration for many cakes. The finished work is shown on page 137, with wedding rings added to complete the arrangement.

1 Cut-out a cardboard template 14.5 × 9 cm (5¾ × 3¾ inches) for the pages. Mix equal quantities of flower paste and sugarpaste, then roll out between guide sticks to ensure it is even. Use a large knife and a guillotine action to cut around the template.

4 Roll out the paste for the cover slightly thicker than required. Give the paste a textured surface by laying embroidery fabric over it, then applying firm pressure. Turn the paste over on a clean cutting board.

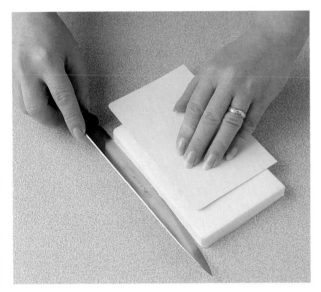

2 Give the edges texture with a sharp knife, leaving the template on the paste to prevent it from being distorted in shape. Leave to dry.

3 Place the book centre on a piece of greaseproof paper and paint the edges with silver food colour. Allow to dry.

5 Use a template measuring about 20.5 × 15 cm (8¼ × 6 inches) for cutting the textured cover. Brush the sugarpaste cover with water. Place the centre pages on one side of the paste and wrap the cover over.

6 Texture the spine of the book with the back of the knife. To indicate that the book is a bible, emboss a cross into the soft paste.

FLOWER SPRAY

1 Make a selection of flowers. Draw the shape of the flower spray on a piece of paper. Tape the flowers together with floristry tape, matching the spray against the pattern as it develops to create the required size and shape. Make 2 identical sprays.

2 Secure a small piece of sugarpaste to the bible with egg white. Push the wires of the sprays firmly into the soft paste.

3 Place another piece of sugarpaste over the wires. Cut the wires of the single flowers to the correct length and gently push them into the sugarpaste.

4 Continue building up the shape of the spray with flowers. Tweezers are very useful for inserting flowers when they are close together. Wires must never penetrate the cake coating, this method is very useful for assembling flowers on a cake.

BASIC RECIPES

The eating-quality of the base cake is equally as important as the finished appearance of the decoration to avoid disappointment. This chart provides quantities for making standard-sized cakes and the method is outlined opposite.

RICH FRUIT CAKE CHART

Total Mixture Weight	470 g (15 oz/scant 1 lb)	1.4 kg (3 lb)	1.9 kg (3¾ lb)	3.3 kg (7¼ lb)	4.7 kg (10¼ lb)
Currants	100 g (3½ oz/⅔ cup)	310 g (10 oz/2 cups)	375 g (12 oz/2½ cups)	670 g (1 lb 5½ oz/6⅓ cups)	970 g (1 lb 15 oz/7¾ cups)
Sultanas (White Raisins)	45 g (1½ oz/3 tbsp)	125 g (4 oz/¾ cup)	155 g (5oz/1 cup)	280 g (9 oz/1½ cups)	400 g (12½ oz/ 2½ cups)
Raisins	45 g (1½ oz/3 tbsp)	125 g (4 oz/¾ cup)	155 g (5 oz/1 cup)	280 g (9 oz/1½ cups)	400 g (12½ oz/2½ cups)
Chopped Mixed Peel	15 g (½ oz/1 tbsp)	60 g (2 oz/⅓ cup)	75 g (2½ oz/⅓ cup plus 1 tbsp)	125 g (4 oz/¾ cup)	170 g (5½ oz/1 cup)
Glacé (Candied) Cherries	30 g (1 oz/2 tbsp)	75 g (2½ oz/⅓ cup plus 1 tbsp)	100 g (3½ oz/½ cup plus 1 tbsp)	200 g (6½ oz/1 cup plus 1 tbsp)	280 g (9 oz/1⅓ cups plus 2 tbsp)
Butter or Margarine	60 g (2 oz/¼ cup)	170 g (5½ oz/⅔ cup)	220 g (7 oz/1 cup)	400 g (12½ oz/1½ cups)	575 g (1 lb 2½ oz/2¼ cups)
Dark Brown Sugar	60 g (2 oz/⅓ cup)	170 g (5½ oz/1 cup)	220 g (7 oz/1⅓ cups)	400 g (12½ oz/2¼ cups)	575 g (1 lb 2½ oz/3⅓ cups)
Eggs	60 g (2 oz/¼ cup)	170 g (5½ oz/⅔ cup)	220 g (7 oz/1 cup)	400 g (12½ oz/1½ cups)	575 g (1 lb 2½ oz/2¼ cups)
Ground Almonds	15 g (½ oz/2 tbsp)	60 g (2 oz/½ cup)	75 g (2½ oz/½ cup plus 2 tbsp)	125 g (4 oz/1¼ cups)	170 g (5½ oz/1⅓ cups plus 2 tbsp)
Plain (All-purpose) Flour	60 g (2 oz/½ cup)	185 g (6oz/1½ cups)	250 g (8 oz/2 cups)	440 g (14 oz/3½ cups)	625 g (1¼ lb/5 cups)
Glycerine	drop	1.25 ml (¼ tsp)	3.75 ml (¾ tsp)	5 ml (1 tsp)	7.5 ml (1½ tsp)
Caramel	drop	1.25 ml (¼ tsp)	3.75 ml (¾ tsp)	5 ml (1 tsp)	7.5 ml (1½ tsp)
Mixed Spice	pinch	1.25 ml (¼ tsp)	2.5 ml (½ tsp)	3.75 ml (¾ tsp)	5 ml (1 tsp)
Cinnamon	pinch	1.25 ml (¼ tsp)	3.75 ml (¾ tsp)	5 ml (1 tsp)	7.5 ml (1½ tsp)

Grated lemon rind and juice, and brandy or rum to taste. For example, use 1 lemon and 60 ml/4 tbsp brandy or rum for the largest cake.

Note: tbsp = tablespoon, tsp = teaspoon

RICH FRUIT CAKE

◆

There is a wide selection of baking tins (pans) available in different shapes and sizes. Many are not standard, so the quantity of cake mixture required has to be calculated individually for each tin. Use the following simple method, remembering that the weight of mixture may vary according to the depth of cake required.

Fill the baking tin with water to about 1 cm (½ inch) below the rim. Weigh the water in the tin: this is more or less equal to the weight of mixture required.

Follow the chart to select the quantities of ingredients which give the weight nearest to your calculated result.

METHOD

◆

Sort and wash the fruit, then leave to dry. Mix the lemon rind and juice with the fruit. Stir in the brandy and rum and cover the bowl, then leave overnight. Line the tin with greaseproof (parchment) paper and grease it well.

Cream the butter and sugar. Slowly add the egg, beating the mixture well. Mix in the caramel and glycerine, then fold in the flour, ground almonds and spices. Do not beat the mixture.

Stir the fruit through the cake mixture, then turn it into the prepared tin and spread it out. Wash, then wet one hand and pat the top of the mixture level.

Bake the cakes at 140°C (275°F/gas 1). The cooking time depends on size and shape. Test by inserting a clean metal skewer in the middle of the cake – if it comes out free of mixture, the cake is cooked. Any mixture on the skewer indicates that the centre of the cake requires longer cooking.

ROYAL ICING

◆

All equipment must be thoroughly clean and free of grease, otherwise the icing will not hold the air which is beaten into it, making it heavy in consistency and unable to hold its shape.

The ratio of ingredients for royal icing are 6:1 of icing sugar to egg white.

Egg White	Icing (Confectioner's) Sugar
30 g (1 oz/6 teaspoons)	185 g (6 oz/1 cup)
90 g (3 oz/⅓ cup plus 3 teaspoons)	545 g (1 lb 2 oz/3⅓ cups)
155 g (5 oz/⅔ cup)	875 g (1¾ lb)
500 g (1 lb/2 cups)	3 kg (6 lb)

METHOD

◆

The egg whites should be at room temperature. Place them in a bowl with three-quarters of the icing sugar. Beat on slow speed for 2 minutes using an electric beater. Adjust the consistency by adding the remaining icing sugar and continue to beat on slow for a further 3 minutes.

Cover the icing with a polythene bag and a damp cloth to prevent the surface from drying and forming a crust.

PROFESSIONAL TIPS

If using egg white powder, reconstitute it in the proportions of 90 g (3 oz/½ cup) to 625 ml (1 pint/ 2½ cups) water.

◆

Throughout the charts, eggs and egg whites are measured by weight rather than by number. This method gives accurate results, particularly when making royal icing.

MEXICAN PASTE

INGREDIENTS
◆

220 g (7 oz/1¼ cups) icing (confectioner's) sugar
15 ml (1 tablespoon) gum tragacanth
5 ml (1 teaspoon) liquid glucose (clear corn syrup)
30 ml (2 tablespoons) cold water

METHOD
◆

Sift the icing sugar and gum tragacanth on a clean work surface and make a well in the middle. Add the liquid glucose and 25 ml (5 teaspoons) of the water.

Gradually mix the ingredients to a paste, adding the extra water if the mixture is too firm. Knead briefly until smooth. Then wrap the paste in a polythene bag and place it in an airtight container.

Excess paste may be wrapped tightly and frozen in an airtight container.

STOCK SYRUP

INGREDIENTS
◆

250 g (8 oz/1 cup) granulated (crystalline) sugar
200 ml (7 fl oz/¾ cup) water

METHOD
◆

Place the sugar and water in a saucepan. Heat gently until the sugar has dissolved, then bring the syrup to the boil. Set aside to cool, then store in clean, covered jars until required.

USE
◆

To stick marzipan to dummies.
To reduce pouring fondant.
To attach sugar flowers to cakes.

FLOWER PASTE

INGREDIENTS
◆

10 ml (2 teaspoons) powdered gelatine
25 ml (5 teaspoons) cold water
10 ml (2 teaspoons) white vegetable fat
10 ml (2 teaspoons) liquid glucose (clear corn syrup)
400 g (12½ oz/2½ cups) icing (confectioner's) sugar
5 ml (1 teaspoon) gum tragacanth
20 ml (4 teaspoons) carboxymethyl cellulose
1 medium egg white

METHOD
◆

Sprinkle the gelatine over the water, then leave to soak for at least an hour. Add the fat and glucose to the soaked gelatine and place over hot water until dissolved. Warm the icing sugar in a cool oven. Warm a mixing bowl and electric beater.

Place the icing sugar, gum tragacanth and carboxymethyl cellulose in the bowl. At this stage the paste is beige and soft; the longer it is mixed the whiter it becomes.

Place the paste in a clean polythene bag, seal this, then put it in an airtight container. Store for 24 hours before use. To use the paste, break off a small piece and knead in extra icing sugar until the paste is elastic. It should 'click' between your fingers as it is kneaded when ready to use.

PROFESSIONAL TIPS

Use good quality gum tragacanth for the best result.
◆
Never put any leftover handled paste back in the container with the fresh paste. Wrap and store leftovers separately.
◆
The paste can be frozen packed in a small airtight container.

EQUIPMENT

ARM REST

This equipment was specially made by my husband. The cross bar may be adjusted to any height to act as a support for the forearms. When working on a cake top, the support helps to steady the hand and avoids damaging finished work by knocking it.

CAKE STAND

Again a specially made item, this is similar to a work bench vice. The round discs revolve for side piping and the foam pads grip the dummy or light-weight cake. This is used mainly for competition work, piped on dummies.

TILTING TURNTABLE

Extremely useful for extension work, this is available from all good suppliers. Not suitable for coating the sides of boards as the supports project upwards.

INDEX